IS Project Management Handbook

2002 Supplement

George M. Doss

PRENTICE HALL
Paramus, NJ 07652

CIP Data Available from Library of Congress

Printed i nthe United States of America

10 9 8 7 6 5 4 3 2 1

ATTENTION: CORPORATIONS AND SCHOOLS

Prentice Hall books are available at quantity discounts with bulk purchase for educational, business, or sales promotional use. For information, please write to: Prentice Hall Special Sales, 240 Frisch Court, Paramus, New Jersey 07652. Please supply: title of book, ISBN, quantity, how to book will be used, date needed.

PRENTICE HALL
Paramus, NJ 07652

On the World Wide Web at http://www.phdirect.com

ACKNOWLEDGMENTS

First, thanks go to two cousins, Jeanette Forrester and Ivaleane Turner, for the support they gave to my mother so I could write this book.

Second, thanks go to two physicians, William R. Sheldon, Jr. and Dennis H. Birenbaum, for their professional support so I could finish this book.

Third, great thanks go to Charles and Rosalie Cook Shipp for the very personal concerns they conveyed so I had the proper attitude to write this book.

Fourth, acknowledgments are given here for the past support given by some very professional people at Prentice Hall: Jacqueline Roulette, Production Editor; Kay Harrison, copyeditor; and Barbara Palumbo, Manager, Electronic Production Services.

In addition, thanks go to John Hiatt, Executive Editor at Prentice Hall, who took this project out of a dark abyss and got it to the light of day quickly. Also thanks to Barbara Morris for her side bars.

DEDICATION

The Road goes ever on and on
      Down from the door where it began.
Now far ahead the Road has gone,
      And I must follow, if I can,
Pursuing it with eager feet,
      Until it joins some larger way
Where many paths and errands meet.
      And whither then? I cannot say.

—Bilbo Baggins of Bag End

The Fellowship of the Ring by J.R.R. Tolkien

Contents

Chapter 29
Reflections on the Checklist Process

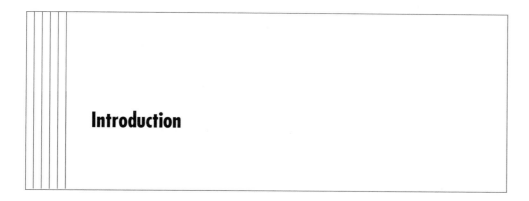

Introduction

HOW THIS SUPPLEMENT WILL HELP YOU

This 2002 Supplement to the *IS Project Management Handbook* is a practical "hands on" resource book that focuses on a process for minimizing invalid time and cost estimates by using data form management. Using the appropriate questionnaires and checklists establishes valid project data parameters, and completing the forms gives comprehensive data for these parameters. When properly utilized, form management can be the primary tool of an excellent quality control and assurance program.

> While the handbook uses "IS" in its title, the uses of IS and IT have blurred significantly. In fact, in the twenty years since James Martin wrote *An Information Systems Manifesto* (Prentice Hall, 1984), managers of information systems and information technology have become synonymous. More importantly, whether you are called an IS manager or an IT manager, when it comes to a project one thing is absolute: The results of a project must be achieved on schedule and on budget.

Anyone involved in networking or Internet projects will find this Supplement useful, not just the project manager. Each chapter gives an explanation and blueprint of the different aspects of project management—from the big-picture project viability evaluation to the details of cost estimates. If you are managing a project—from the relatively uncomplicated addition of hardware, to the integration of a new application, to the major redesign of a network such as a change from a client/server paradigm to an object-oriented paradigm—then this Supplement can be of great use.

"Garbage in, garbage out" is more than a cliché; it is a statement about the harsh reality of project management. This saying could be applied to two of the major causes of a project's failure: 1) invalid data for time estimates and 2) cost estimates. The third cause is poor management. In a well-run project, project management is an integrated process that assists in achieving the only goal of any project manager; i.e., to complete the measurable goals on schedule and on budget.

In any project there are two primary groupings: management activity groups and procedural groups. The first focuses on such basic tasks as Internet access, system security, or risk management in a complex environment. The second—traditional project management—was originally developed around the procedural groups that carried out planning, designing, developing, testing, and implementing. In both, quality control and assurance has evolved from a specific group of tasks into a set of tasks that impacts the whole project and cannot be ignored by any activity group or procedural grouping.

The Supplement focuses on the design and development process of project forms. Included are discussions of the six basic steps for identifying data types and their related data for any project management form or checklist, and its associated instructions. Examples of data types are time and cost estimates, but examples of data are the specific values of the time and cost estimates. These six steps identify:

1. Why a form should exist

2. What should be asked and collected

3. Who should design and develop the form

4. Where the form should be designed, developed, and used

5. When the form should be designed and developed

6. How the form should be designed and developed

The Supplement emphasizes the first, second, and sixth steps. The other three steps are discussed when appropriate, but the responses to these steps can only be determined within the context of local issues and organization. Using the simple six-step identification or query process, you can design and develop project management forms or checklists and instructions; their successful implementation will give you a competitive advantage in the marketplace.

A fundamental premise of the "how" step is that any project management form or checklist should include the parameters (optimistic, realistic, or pessimistic estimates) to the data requirements. In each chapter, there is a discussion of some general and specific consequences and benefits for not using the example form created because of the discussion. The forms are collected in Chapter 28A for ease of comparison and reference. The forms as a whole reflect a ten-step project management process and, at a high level, a parallel data form management process.

The Supplement expands on the general framework of the basic steps for project management outlined in the original book:

- Project evaluating
- Scope planning and defining
- Activity planning and sequencing
- Resource planning
- Time estimating
- Schedule developing
- Cost estimating
- Budget developing
- Quality controlling
- Risk managing

There is a discussion of the need for the project manager and the team to consider the full process in the design and development of a project's goals and tasks. Some areas might be completed quickly; if so, the only response required is: "There are no tasks required for this area."

Any IS or IT management professional can use this Supplement to formulate project data types and data, using the examples. The handbook begins with the methodology for using the technique of playing the "20 questions" game. The integrated answers should clearly give a "yes" or "no" response to the question, "Is this project viable?"

Data management begins the moment you consider the viability of a project, not after you have started it. Perhaps the most critical project data are those that identify whether or not a project is viable. You need to know such data as the sources and availability of funds, general skill requirements, and their availability.

DESIGNING AND DEVELOPING FORMS

The information in this supplement can assist you in addressing the concerns and challenges of project form management—data control and assurance. Although the supplement is not as comprehensive as the original book, it discusses all the major components of the process and offers new material not found in the original book, as well as real-life examples of successes and failures.

This "hands on" guide boosts your knowledge of form management and shows how to incorporate this procedure into your company's operations. The core concept underlying both books is that "Project management needs to be an identified and organized process based on measurable goals that can be clearly explained to the customer."

An example of the general direction of this supplement is that, in using the definitions given in each chapter, you could create a set of data types for capturing data that will help you make judicious estimates for any project activity, task, hardware, or software as follows:

Estimate	Optimistic	Realistic	Pessimistic
Cost	_____	_____	_____
Time	_____	_____	_____
Equipment	_____	_____	_____
Material	_____	_____	_____
Skill	_____	_____	_____

This simple framework could be put on index cards and used in activity planning. For a more complex application, you could put this framework in a spreadsheet and electronically tabulate data by categories. This information is fundamental to completing PERT—Program Evaluation and Review Technique—a utility that should only be used to manage a very complex project. Thus, this book tries to reflect the use of data types and data over the broadest rangefrom index card to PERT.

Besides the uses of "data type" in a specific manner, there are three other special usages. First, "hunk of data" means a policy, standard, or set of procedures. Second, "byte of data" means descriptive data such as data on a piece of hardware. Third, "bit of data" means a single fact such as a unique name for a function.

Project management incorporates a set of guiding functions such as planning, designing, developing, controlling, and implementing. Its broad set of standards includes the fundamental principle that you must have measurable goals that are managed in an organized manner. Project management benchmarks are headed by the invocation to "be on schedule and on budget," although that usually translates as "do it in less time than stated and significantly under cost." The prosect management process may have a script, but in reality there is more ad-libbing than reciting. All of these ideas must be used in the process of identifying reliable project management data types, and the creating of forms and checklists that adequately capture the data implied from the data types.

THE SUPPLEMENT'S ORGANIZATION

Section 1A of this Supplement follows the organization of Section 1 of the *IS Project Management Handbook*. The expansion of each of the original chapters is concerned with data form management or data control and assurance as an integral program for project management activities and procedures.

Section 1A focuses on the design and development process, using the six-step identification process in the context of the ten areas of the project management process. Essential definitions established in the *IS Project Management Handbook* are used as the basis for the design and development of a questionnaire or checklist for the specific area of discussion.

In addition, each of these ten chapters contain approximately seven subsections:

- Objectives
- Form rationale
- Essential definitions
- Supportive definitions
- Data type refinement process
- Form and checklist development process
- Chapter 28A

Sections 2 through 4 of the original handbook are not supplemented at this time.

Section 5A includes Chapter 28A, which has ten example questionnaires and checklists based on the data types discussed in Section 1A. In addition, the forms have instructions—explaining how the form will be completed and what items are mandatory or optional—that serve as a standard and as a benchmark for expected data. When you only have a name as a label for a block on a form, the instructions should give complete expectations for the data description. In addition, it is easier to change the set of instructions than the form when you find you are not getting the expected data.

The final chapter (Chapter 29) summarizes the major ideas put forth in Section 1A, including a brief discussion of the impact of skill sets on the form and checklist development process.

Any form or checklist you develop is determined by your management skill sets. "Skill set" means not a single skill such as a writing skill, but a group of skills that can be collectively labeled, such as organizer, negotiator, facilitator, or salesperson. For more information on skill sets, see the author's *Management Skills for IT Professionals* (Prentice Hall, 2001).

A final thought: Invalid time and cost estimates are the basic reasons for the need for crisis management. This Supplement approaches crises with the following ideas under consideration:

- A crisis is never a single event; it is always a multitude of events that can seriously affect (read as *terminate*) a project.
- A crisis may begin as a misperception rather than a real perception.

Ideally, a project manager will not need to deal with crisis-level management during his or her tour of duty on any project, but if the unavoidable occurs, this Supplement should help bring the crisis into focus and thereby point the manager toward a solution.

> While there is duplication of definitions and ideas throughout the book, they should be read in context rather than as just restatements. For example, "logistics" is not just discussed in one place, but throughout Section 1A. Also, once you read the Supplement from cover to cover, ideally you will use it as a reference.

The 2002 Supplement indirectly uses the concepts from an object-oriented paradigm rather than a client/server paradigm. A client can be a server and vice versa.

Section 1A

Managing Forms for the IS Project

This section discusses the procedures for defining data using a form or a checklist as the foundation for valid cost and time estimates and a reliable quality control program. Proper practices should minimize the consequences of any invalid (poorly defined) estimates.

The technique of playing the "20 questions" game of "Is this project viable?" as formulated in Chapter 1A is used as a framework for the discussions throughout this section. Chapter 28A, "Example Forms, Checklists, and Instructions," contains example forms or checklists with their appropriate instructions.

- Chapter 1A: *Evaluating Project Viability* gives a process for developing a set of 20 questions that resolve whether a project is viable or not.

- Chapter 2A: *Defining and Creating a Scope Plan* shows a process for developing a form or a checklist that can be used to establish project goals and performance benchmarks.

- Chapter 3A: *Creating and Managing an Activity Plan* discusses a process for developing a form or a checklist that can be used to develop an activity plan and the criteria for a valid activity sequence.

- Chapter 4A: *Identifying and Estimating Project Resources* formulates a process for developing a form or a checklist that can be used to write a resource plan and the measurable criteria for the resources.

- Chapter 5A: *Creating Manageable Time Estimates* defines a process for developing a form or a checklist that can be used to create reliable time estimates and measurable criteria for time estimates.

- Chapter 6A: *Creating a Schedule* illustrates a process for developing a form or a checklist that can be used to create a flexible schedule based on reliable time estimates.

- Chapter 7A: *Evaluating and Estimating Cost* discusses a process for developing a form or a checklist that can be used to create reliable cost estimates and measurable criteria for cost estimates.

- Chapter 8A: *Defining and Managing a Project Budget* illustrates a process for developing a form or a checklist that can be used to create a flexible budget based on reliable time estimates used to create a schedule and then cost estimates.

- Chapter 9A: *Managing Quality Control and Assurance* gives a process for developing a form or a checklist that can be used to manage a comprehensive quality control and assurance program based on standards and benchmarks.

- Chapter 10A: *Managing Risk* establishes a process for developing a form or a checklist that can be used to manage an aggressive risk-management program based on valid measurable criteria.

The boxed text shows real-time business examples

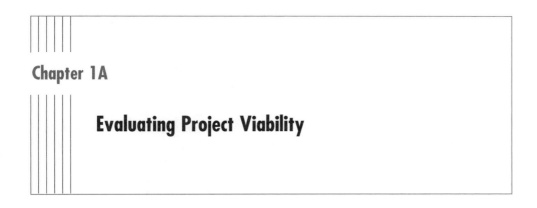

Chapter 1A

Evaluating Project Viability

OBJECTIVES: At the end of this chapter, you will be able to:

- Identify seven critical benefits for using an evaluation for project viability.
- State the definition for a metaquestion.
- Identify 50 concepts that are associated with a discussion on project viability.
- Build knowledge for developing a set of 20 questions that determine the viability of a potential project.
- Use 20 project viability questions to create a "yes-no" checklist with instructions for a discussion with a project initiator.

One of the fundamental aspects of a project in the pre-proposal stage is the need for adequate research. Evaluating a project with a checklist and metaquestions helps to answer many of the issues that the successful project manager will integrate into the bigger picture with the help of upper management. But if management fails to properly evaluate the market and scope of the project, success may well be out of reach.

For example, several years ago a large B2B medical supplier decided to catch the Internet wave and launch a Web site that, in theory, would make it easier for their clients to make purchases. Their project failed on several critical fronts.

First, the marketing department had neglected to ascertain the fact that, doctors, for example, seem to be too busy to use the Internet while at work and tend to make their purchases using existing CRM (Customer

Relationship Management) programs. They have little interest in or time to learn how to use a new technology.

Secondly, the site build was outsourced to a Web company that promised short development time and complete software integration. But the project leaders — there were two in succession — should have first established that the Web builders could handle the project. The builders could not figure out how to get the shopping cart to work with the point-of-sale software and the site crashed on the day of the soft launch. Their last-ditch solution was to suggest a million-dollar middleware purchase, which the IT people at the medical supply company researched and discovered was unnecessary. Eventually, the site was rebuilt by in-house talent, and the launch was pushed back a year. The Web builders did quite well, because 75% of their fee had been paid up front.

What could or should have been done? The project manager, along with upper management, should have researched the pros and cons of in-house versus outsourced development, using a project viability evaluation form. In retrospect, the site could have been done just with in-house talent and with a longer development cycle.

USING A PROJECT VIABILITY EVALUATION

A project viability evaluation is a risk virus vaccine. Note that the following is an example of how you might prepare the evaluation form; its parameters will depend on your formulation, using 20 questions that clarify the particular customer's objective. If you cannot resolve your concerns in 20 questions, you need to review and revise your premises. In addition, a 20-question evaluation helps the customer clarify the problem and shows the customer that you have a formal project process. A positive result can be used to gain upper management's buy-in.

The two leading questions should look something like this:

- What funding exists for this project?
- What are the project's measurable objectives?

If the answer to the first question is negative or unknown, you might have a conversation with the customer, but not a negotiation. If the customer does have a potential figure in mind, then that becomes the point of negotiation for the response to the second question.

Even when the answers are negative or unknown, however you should continue the conversation through the other 18 questions. The answers to these questions may actually lead to a positive response.

This kind of project manager/customer dialogue can provide the project team with a realistic scenario for making their estimates. Also, the project team can use the responses as a foundation for essential project documents such as the Scope Plan, Activity Plan, Project Schedule, and Project Budget.

I have seen only one project succeed when there was not a clear definition of funding. The corporation wanted to become ISO-compliant (International Organization for Standardization) for internal and external benefits. It was thought that using the ISO process would save money in product design, development, and testing. More importantly, it would generate new business.

ASKING THE CORRECT QUESTIONS

The broadest questions for developing any set of project evaluation questions are of course:

1. How?
2. Why?
3. When?
4. Where?
5. Who?
6. What?

These questions are labeled *metaquestions*, which means first-ordered questions. They are the broadest and simplest questions you can ask; of themselves, they are also the most ineffective. They are the first categorical steps toward clarification or refinement. How-type questions involve methodology (tasks and activities as discussed in Chapter 3A), skill prerequisites, and financial concerns (that is, cost estimates and budget which are discussed in detail in Chapters 7A and 8A). Why-type questions involve justifications such as cost-benefit analysis, customer expectations, benchmarks, standards, and especially measurable project goals. Questions on benchmarks and standards are important to the quality control assurance process and the risk management program discussed in Chapters 9A and 10A. When-type questions involve time estimates and a schedule, which are discussed in more detail in Chapters 5A and 6A. Where-type questions consider location definitions, and resource prerequisites. Who-type questions involve primarily skill types and level prerequisites, and the responsible agents. What-type questions involve resources (skills, equipment, materials, and project duration; that is, production time plus wait time. Resource questions are discussed in Chapter 4A.

The first step in using metaquestions is to narrow them down using categorical statements that include the characteristics, functions, and goals of a project, such as a specific customer definition rather than global customer definition. The second step is classifying a potential project in terms of what is and what is not — the foundation of the forms for a project Scope Plan (Chapter 2A.) These statements are then turned into questions based on the "Big Six."

This process helps ensure as risk-free an environment as possible. Then, you finally ask the question "Is the project viable?," the response will be a clear "yes" or "no."

USING ESSENTIAL TERMS

The following 50 terms are essential to a full discussion of any project and form the supports for the framework of this book. Beyond these terms, you must also consider local technical concepts; that is, software, hardware, and infrastructure.

Not only visual objects define a system's infrastructure in a networking system, but by such concepts as interoperability, portability, and scalability.

An **assumption** is a prediction that something will be true, either an action or an event that ensures project success.

Authority is the investment in managing and controlling a series of tasks such as a project. For example, the critical statement the strategic manager has to make is: "The project manager has the authority to make all decisions required to achieve a successful project."

A **benchmark** is a specific technical level of excellence.

A **checklist** is an organized list, possibly a standard of action, that usually has to be followed in sequence to accomplish a specified goal. However, a checklist can be as simple as a set of options for answering the question: "Have I considered the following items for this activity or task?"

A **constraint** is a parameter, limitation, or a boundary for the project plan such as the Budget or the Schedule.

A **consultant** is a person from outside the normal resource pool with experience in solving a specific project issue. The consultant usually works from a biased position.

Control is the monitoring of progress and the checking for variances in the plan.

A **cost-benefit analysis** is the development of a ratio to determine if a project is financially viable.

A **critical activity** or task if not completed means project failure.

A **deliverable** is a clearly defined project result, product or service.

An **estimate** is a guess based on opinion, or a forecast based on experience. Cost, time, and resource estimates are the foundations for project planning.

Expectation is a stated project goal that can become a perceived undocumented result.

Goal characteristics have to be measurable, specific, and potentially possible.

Information system project management is a documented parallel process within a set schedule, and within a defined budget, with available resources and skills to achieve defined user expectations for a networking environment. The networking environment's primary function is to transmit data among users.

Innovation is a significant change or breakthrough.

Interoperability is to what degree the various network components work with each other successfully.

Logistics is the process of getting the correct resource to the correct location at the correct time.

Management is the process of working with people, resources, equipment, and materials to achieve organizational goals.

Management team is a supervisory team that coordinates broad issues that affect the corporation.

The **Market Analysis Report** documents and verifies market opportunities and justifies the features, services, and applications for the project goals.

A **model** is a theoretical environment with as much data as possible to reflect reality adequately for decision-making.

An **objective** is a set of measurable goals to achieve a defined target, if not achieved, has critical results.

An **opportunity** is a situation that will positively affect the project in time, money, resources, or all three in a significant manner.

An **organization** is an entity created to achieve what the separate individuals could not accomplish.

Portability is a characteristic of software. It is the degree to which the software can be transferred from one environment to another.

Process is a systematic and sequential set of activities (tasks) to achieve a set of measurable goals.

A **program** is a type of recurring project, such as the annual budget, not to be confused with a set of programming code.

A **project** is an organized set of tasks to reach a measurable outcome within a specified duration.

Project management has many aliases including program management, product management, and construction management. In all cases, it is the managing, controlling, and integrating of tasks, resources, time and costs to achieve defined measurable outcomes within a specified duration.

The **project manager** is the person with overall responsibility for managing and controlling the project tasks (defined and undefined) to achieve a measurable outcome within a specified schedule and budget.

A **project team** is an organization that is put together to achieve a specific set of measurable goals within a specific time and with limited resources, equipment, and materials.

Quality assurance is based on performance. It is the establishing of performance standards, then measuring and evaluating and measuring project performance against these standards. It is the component of quality management that considers project performance deviations.

> From the beginning of the project the project manager should confirm that the Quality Assurance team enjoys good communications with all members of the project team that will be supplying QA with documentation. This process ensures accurate testing and improved functionality.

Quality control is the component of quality management that considers the system or development processes of a project. It is the tasks used to meet standards through the gathering of performance information, inspecting, monitoring, and testing.

A **realistic estimate** is an assumption that there will probably be a few difficulties, but with compromise, the difficulties will be overcome.

A **resource** is anything that supports the project. This includes, in general terms, money, skills, materials, time, facilities, and equipment.

Resource planning is establishing support requirements for a project as to costs, availability, start-date and end-date (length of time for use plus duration), and technical specifications.

A **risk** is a performance error that can have a significant or disastrous impact on the success of a project or major activity. It is more than a problem; its effect can have an adverse or disastrous consequence on the project's outcome.

Scalability is to what degree a network can be enhanced without a major change in design.

The **Schedule** is the duration of the project, including production time and wait time. It is also a production plan for the allocation of tasks with deadlines.

Scope is the amount of work and resources (skills, materials, and equipment) required for project completion.

Skill level is a factor used by a project manager in planning the project's Budget, rather than using a headcount.

Specific goals are project goals that are measurable, unambiguous, and match exactly the customer's stated expectations.

The **sponsor** is the one who provides the resources and the working environment to make possible the achievement of project goals.

A **stakeholder** is any person or organization interested in the project. This includes the customer, your boss, you, the team, and interested government regulators.

A **standard** is usually an external, industry-accepted document for achieving quality for one or more of the project-defined expected goals.

A **Statement of Work** (SOW) is an integrated set of descriptions as to project tasks, goals, risks, and resources to complete a measurable outcome.

A **strategic manager** heads an area of a corporation that includes the IS project as a part of that person's performance goals.

A **system** is an interactive set of tasks or groups that form a whole with dynamics that impact all the components.

The **tactical manager** is the one responsible for the overall flow of the project process so that the strategic goals are met.

The **Third-Party Market Agreement** provides the plans whereby the project or a part of the project is to be the responsibility of a third-party developer.

ADDING SUPPORTIVE TERMS

Any other term used in Chapters 2A through 10A is supportive to the long list of essential terms. More than 200 terms are defined throughout this book and all are included in the glossary. These defined terms are discussed in more detail in *IS Project Management Handbook* and *Management Skills for IT Professionals* (Prentice Hall, 2000).

> Some of the definitions are duplicated in other chapters, but their contextual meaning may vary according to how you use the book — whether as a reference guide or as a textbook.

DETERMINING PROJECT VIABILITY

On your first try do not expect to have 20 questions ready to determine a project's viability; this is only a suggested technique based on the old game that begins with the question, "Is it living or non-living?" The format establishes two contrasting points and requires a "yes" or "no" answer. Perhaps, the first question you could ask is: "Are there measurable goals?" If the answer is "yes," then the second question you might ask is: "Are sufficient funds available to complete the customer's measurable goals?"

The 20-question game is immediately over if the first question is "no." You should never go to upper management to discuss a project without measurable project goals; instead, you might discuss an opportunity with upper management if there are no measurable goals.

You can use the 20-question game in two situations. First, with no measurable goals, an opportunity can be discussed in terms of its future possibilities. Second, with measurable goals, you can determine if you have the capabilities (skills) and resources (especially time and funding) to successfully complete the project on schedule and on budget.

Before discussing a project's viability with upper management, you might brainstorm with some of your staff and those who would be involved in the project. Brainstorming is an excellent technique for generating ideas or suggestions that can be later ordered in a rational sequence. Do not get hung up on the order of the goals, unless one or more are critical to all the others. If this is the case, then you have the basis for using the critical path method at a later point; that is, when calculating activity and time estimates.

The following brief list of questions is not definitive, but shows the kinds of questions you could ask when brainstorming:

- How complete is the list of measurable goals?
- Why should this project be done?
- How much funding is required to complete the critical goals and any other goals?
- What types of tasks and skills are required?
- When are the goals to be completed?
- When are management tools required?
- What are the required benchmarks and standards?
- Who has tactical responsibility for the project?
- What are the potential impacts on the system's infrastructure?
- How can potential risks be determined?

Below are 10 questions in the "yes-no" response format for the project viability process:

- Are there measurable project goals?
- Is there sufficient justification (cost-benefit analysis, customer relationship, or general market environment) to begin this project?
- Is there sufficient funding?
- Does the present staff have the skills to achieve the defined potential tasks?
- Can the goals be achieved within the expected duration (time)?
- Are the necessary management tools available, and are there appropriate skilled personnel available?
- Have the implications for possible benchmarks and standards been considered?
- Is there a written statement of tactical responsibility?
- Are there any critical impacts on the system's infrastructure?
- Have criteria of potential risks been established?

While some of the above questions might not be completely answered at a meeting on project viability, they should be able to be answered with a high degree of probability.

USING A CHECKLIST AND FORM DEVELOPMENT PROCESS

The following set of 20 project questions in the pre-proposal phase could be used to create a checklist that reflects a set of "yes-no" responses and to develop a local template. This process is a requirement for any discussion of project viability with upper management.

> In Chapter 28A, there is a checklist and instructions for creating and using project viability questions (01viable and 01viabi).

1.   **What are the measurable project goals?**

The active word is "measurable." If you do not have measurable goals, you are building your project process on sand and you only need to wait for the first tide (risk) to wash you out to the depths of failure.

2.   **What potential materials and equipment are available?**

At this point you should have some sense of the requirements for the types of materials and equipment to be used for each goal.

3.   **What and where are available resources?**

You need to know what the resources are and where they are available. You might find resources outside the IS group or even outside the corporation in the case of a consultant. If some resources are not immediately available, you will need to determine if they are critical to the project's success.

4.   **How do possible project costs compare to project benefits?**

You should do at least a basic cost-benefit analysis so that you can present the results to upper management and justify or not justify the project's viability.

5. Why should this project be done?

Without specific justification, how can you get approval to do the project? You may need more than the customer wants or has the funds to do. This scenario is potentially fraught with danger.

6. What and when are appropriate skills available?

You need to have measurable and specific skill-level descriptions that include technical requirements.

7. How will the project's budget items be funded?

Unfortunately, budget items for a given project are probably scattered over a number of different budgets. You need to create a project budget even if it is outside of the formal financial structure so that you can manage the entire process.

8. What and where are the required project management tools for achieving project results?

Project management tools can be as simple as a set of index cards or as complex as a utility that can manage a project based on PERT (Performance Evaluation and Review Technique). Remember, the more complex a tool, the greater the learning curve. Garbage in is garbage out no matter how sophisticated the management tool. The problem is that the more complex the tool, the harder it is to identify the garbage.

9. What benchmarks and standards have been identified in the quality control and assurance program for the deliverables?

It is critical that you identify required standards and benchmarks to ensure the success of any project that requires quality management. Remember that a quality deliverable means customer satisfaction.

10. How do the project goals reflect efficiency and innovation?

Because something may be a buzz word on your or the customer's tongue does not mean it is tasty. You do need to consider how the project's goals will impact the IS infrastructure and its efficiency and how any innovation or enhancement will ripple through the system.

11. What are the critical assumptions and constraints for managing the project's goals?

There is only one rule at this point: You MUST define them.

12. Who should have written tactical authority for the project's management?

If you are going to be a project manager, you must have written authority to do what is legally necessary to complete a project on schedule and on budget. This authorization should come from the upper management level. You cannot begin a project without this legitimization.

13. How do deliverables relate to the project goals?

You need to have a list of deliverables associated with each goal; these could include training or special documentation. You might also consider the types of presentations that have to be delivered as each goal is developed and completed.

14. How stable is the technology required to achieve project results?

You need a set of assumptions and constraints that relate to any technology to be used in the development of deliverables. Introducing a new technology during the project duration could create a devastating ripple effect.

15. How will the results impact the return on investments (ROI)?

ROI as used here is more that a simple cost-benefit analysis. ROI impact might mean a significant improvement in your system scalability in a given area, so that your customer would be very satisfied.

16. How realistic are the deadlines to achieve project results?

There is only one rule at this point: you MUST have realistic deadlines. You should not be expected to start a project the day after it is approved by your management and your customer because complex issues need to be resolved first.

17. What are the events that could cause the project to fail?

You manage risks by considering them before they happen. This activity is a part of defining assumptions and constraints.

18. What are the events that can make the project successful?

You must not ignore the positive. The project may be happening at the correct time and in the correct place.

19.   What are the possible impacts of the end results on the information system?

Because you are an IS manager, you must filter all data through the defined goals of your group.

20.   What are the criteria for the various types of estimates?

Remember, any estimate comes in three flavors — pessimistic, realistic, and optimistic, so you need to determine the basic project cost and time estimates in each of these three flavors. You will also need to describe your potential skill requirements in the same manner.

At the pre-proposal survey step, you are not looking for details or precise data except in a few areas, but you do need to establish clear parameters. As in football, you must first establish the playing area, the goal posts, the end field, and the yardage lines. If you are managing the creation of an XML-based application for defining a financial database for corporate budget items, you will need data that can be determined from

- What are the budget items?
- When is the database to be accessed?
- Where is the database located?
- Why does the application for the database need to be XML-based?
- Who is to access the database?
- How is the database to be accessed?

Just by using the metaquestions, you can quickly establish the types of data you need in this critical area. Other critical areas include:

- Sources of funding
- Basic assumptions and constraints
- Potential impact, especially on the system's infrastructure
- Potential possibilities for risks and opportunities.
- Technological requirements

The development of any checklist or form should begin by asking questions about the project. In such a case, you must consider the potential rather than the actual.

> The checklist and instructions in Chapter 28A are examples only. Based on your situation, you will need to create your own set of questions. Comprehending how to create your 20 questions is more important using an example.
>
> 01viable — Checklist for Project Viability Questions
>
> 01viabi — Instructions for Using a Viability Checklist

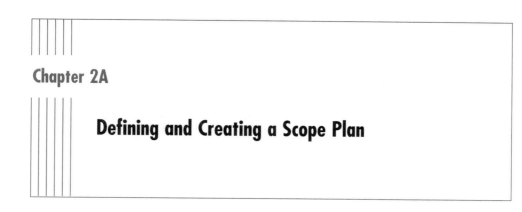

Chapter 2A

Defining and Creating a Scope Plan

OBJECTIVES: At the end of this chapter, you will be able to:

- Recognize that without a clearly written Scope Plan, you establish a risk type usually referred to as "scope creep."

- Identify 104 concepts that are relevant to the development of a checklist to be used to create data types for a Scope Plan.

- Develop a very basic skill level to use as part of an interrogative process for creating or enhancing data requirements for a Scope Plan.

- Be familiar with how to develop an outline form that can refine and enhance a data type and data survey for a Scope Plan.

When a term such as *Scope Plan* is used in Chapters 2A through 10A, it is a title for a specific document used in managing a project.

In a recent television commercial, a small group of people huddles around an office computer screen. They watch intently as a colleague at the keyboard raises his hand and strikes the "enter" key. Everyone stares at the screen with an air of intense anticipation. On-screen a counter registers their first sale and the employees let out a collective sigh of relief. Then more sales register and the small crowd cheers. But within moments the counter spins wildly out of control as thousands of sales click on the screen. Silently, their expressions change from elation to panic as the small group realizes that the have just been buried alive by success.

> This wickedly funny commercial about scalability issues related to e-commerce is an excellent example of a disaster scenario that a competent project manager plans for from the first day of the job. And the Scope Plan is the tool to create to manage the type and the flow of data throughout the project, as well as to plan for the results of the project.

DETERMINING VALID DATA TYPES AND DATA

Frequently the phrase "scope creep" is used to express a problem of project management. Creep implies a very slow movement. Actually, the phrase might be better phrased as "scope earthquake." When there is a poorly defined Scope Plan without measurable objectives and without associated procedural standards and performance benchmarks there is a potential risk that is like an earthquake — hidden, sudden, destructive, and deadly.

Without a well-defined Scope Plan and its support documents such as the Business Justification, there is not an objective baseline for negotiations on customer expectations, valid cost and time estimates, and workable schedule and budget.

Chapter 28A includes an example form of 20 survey questions, plus instructions that you must consider five additional variants for each question. The survey is used to get the assessable assumptions and constraints for defining valid estimates (cost, time, and resources) and parameters of the project. The form is based on the terms and procedures discussed in this chapter to get a set of data types and data used in the Scope Plan to stop "creep."

> WARNING: If you think you do not have time to use the form, recognize your house (project) is being built on sand with the tide coming in rapidly. Would you feel comfortable to travel to an unknown location by the shortest route without the use of a map? The Scope Plan is a map; you have to decide how precise the map needs to be so you are either a project manager or a project firefighter.

The Scope Plan sets the "mode" or "manner" for all of the other project documents. It is the standard and the benchmark for all of these documents.

USING ESSENTIAL TERMS

While there are a number of terms important to this discussion, three terms are essential.

The **Scope Plan** is the strategic view of the constraints and assumptions of the project as developed by the project team.

A **constraint** is a parameter, limitation, or a boundary for the project plan such as the Budget or the Schedule.

An **assumption** is a prediction that something will be true, either an action or an event that ensures project success, such as, "There will be identified potential risks, but somehow they will be overcome."

> Any term discussed in Chapters 3A through 10A is fundamental to a full discussion of the Scope Plan. Some 250 terms are discussed in Chapters 1A through 10A.

ADDING SUPPORTIVE TERMS

Besides the three essential concepts given above, following are an additional 101 terms, concepts, and document definitions. Some of these terms are essential to discussions in later chapters. In some cases it is not the detail that is important such as with the documents noted, but the parameters for developing these documents. Details or new data are actually added to many of the documents because of project milestones or even for unforeseen change.

Several important project management organizations are listed for your consideration. You may have to simply state in the Scope Plan that something has been considered and there is no further need for more details because of specific reasons. This action preserves for history your earliest justifications for the project's direction.

> So many concepts and terms are given here because the Scope Plan is the framework or foundation for the whole project.

An **activity** at the operational level (a task at the tactical level) is the effort required to achieve a measurable result that uses time and resources.

An **audit** is a formal study of the project as a whole, or a project's component, as to status (progress and results), costs, and procedures.

Authority is the investment in managing and controlling a series of tasks such as a project.

A **baseline plan** is the initial approved point from which any deviations will be determined using standards and benchmarks.

A **benchmark** is a specific technical level of excellence.

The **Budget** is a plan where costs are organized into debits and credits (expenses and revenues). It is a formal plan that uses a chart of accounts to give structure to estimates for expenses and revenues.

The **Business Affiliate Plan** provides information when the project or a part of the project is to be the responsibility of a third-party developer.

The **Business Justification** is the general rationale for making the financial investment.

A **checklist** is an organized list, possibly a standard of action that usually has to be followed in sequence to accomplish a specified goal. However, a checklist can be as simple as a set of options for answering the question "Have I considered the following items for this activity or task?"

The **Commercial Specification** is an evolution of the Business Justification. It identifies the market need and gives adequate requirement and limitation data for the design and development group(s).

Without appropriate market research, the project is probably destined to fail. One well-known Internet company failed to keep an eye on 'Net market trends and began an affiliate marketing project when affiliate marketing was already dead on the 'Net. The heavy investment required to get the project off the ground was part of the financial drain that brought the company to its knees.

Communication is oral or written transfer of data or information between individuals.

Communications is the process of getting the correct data to the correct person at the correct time in a cost-effective mode.

Communications is one of the most fundamental issues that a project manager has to address. Some traditional communications tools are white board diagrams and weekly up-date meetings, while other collaboration tools (software) can be provided on a company intranet to allow people to share documents and discuss issues. Whichever tools are used, they should be readily available to all project members as well as to any managers involved in the project.

A **confidence level** is the acceptance level of risk usually determined statistically by a percentage of time or cost.

A **consultant** is a person from outside the normal resource pool with experience on solving a specific project issue. The consultant usually works from a biased position.

The **Content Agreement** is the written "contract" between the development group and the marketing group as to the content and functions of the project.

Contingency is the rational preparation for change.

Corporate values are a common set of beliefs held by the corporate stakeholders about their business environment.

A **cost-benefit analysis** is the development of a ratio to determine if a project is financially viable.

A **critical activity** or task, if not completed, means project failure.

A **critical path** is when there is no available time for the slippage of the activity or task (no slack time).

A **cross-functional team** is the most common type of team for a corporate IS project, and includes many technical and support groups with a multiple set of skills, ideas, goals, attitudes, and so forth.

The **Customer Documentation Strategy** provides how timely, high-quality project documentation becomes available. There really is a triad in quality: control and assurance, documentation, and training.

A **deliverable** is a clearly defined project result, product, or service.

Dependency means that a task has to be completed before a succeeding task can be completed. For example, coding has to be completed before code testing can be completed.

The **Design and Development Plan** drives the project Integration Plan that captures all major design and development deliverables and milestones for management tracking and reporting.

An **estimate** is a guess based on opinion, or a forecast based on experience. Cost, time, and resource estimates are the foundations for project planning.

An **event** is a point in time such as the start or end of an activity or a task.

Expectation is a stated project goal that can become a perceived undocumented result.

Feedback an activity that should be held on a regular basis, is where the status of the person being evaluated can be clearly stated based on measurable standards or benchmarks.

The **Field Introduction Requirements** document reflects the strategy and detailed plans to verify conformance to specification and functionality as defined in the Project Specification.

A **gate** is another term for milestone or a major project event.

Goal characteristics have to be measurable, specific, and potentially possible.

A **group** is two or more individuals with corporate identity that is considered an entity.

Headcount is a factor used by business managers in planning an annual budget, but should not be used by project managers.

The **Initial Budget Estimates** provides a view of the expected developmental costs. Estimates are usually based on the Preliminary Project Specification. This document is updated in the Project Cost Update.

The **Initial Funding Requirements** document is for monitoring and reporting project costs at each major phase of implementation. It should include comparisons to the original funding document used to establish financial targets and expected milestones and deliverables. This document can also be included in the Project Cost Update.

The **International Organization for Standardization** (ISO) is a consortium that sets standards in a variety of areas.

Interoperability is the degree to which the various network components work with each other successfully.

ISO 9000 is a quality system standard for any product, service, or process.

ISO 9001 is a quality system standard for design, production, and installation of a product or service.

ISO 9002 is a quality system model for quality assurance in production and installation.

ISO 9003 is a quality system model for quality assurance in final inspection and testing.

ISO 9004 is a set of quality management guidelines for any organization to use to develop and implement a quality system.

A **learning curve** is a graphical representation of repetitive tasks that when done on a continuous basis lead to a reduction in activity duration, resources, and costs.

Logistics is the process of getting the correct resource to the correct location at the correct time.

A **management review** is a regularly scheduled performance review.

The **Market Analysis Report** documents and verifies market opportunities and justifies the features, services, and applications for the project goals.

A **milestone** is a clearly defined date of start or 100 percent completion.

A **model** is a theoretical environment with as much data as possible to reflect reality adequately for decision-making.

A **node** is a network event that is achieved or is not achieved. A milestone is a node type.

An **objective** is a set of measurable goals to achieve a defined target, if not achieve, has critical results.

An **operational manager** is a person that handles the day-to-day operations or activities for a specific functional group or area that has been defined in the project plan.

An **opportunity** is a situation that will positively affect the project in time, money, resources, or all three in a significant manner.

An **organization chart** is normally a visual representation of who reports to whom. It shows the hierarchical and perhaps functional relationships among organizational groups. The project organization chart must include the core project responsibilities of each team member.

Organizational culture is a common set of assumptions, principles, processes, and structures held or used by members of a corporation, company, or even a project team.

Padding is an informal action, such as adding time or cost to an estimate, that should not take place. Any such estimates should be formalized in a contingency plan.

Performance is the measurable level of action to achieve a measurable project goal. It is the act or level of work demonstrated and judged based on identified skill level.

A **phase** is a project segment such as planning, designing, and developing.

PMI stands for the Project Management Institute, a professional organization that studies and promotes project management.

Portability is a characteristic of software. It is the degree to which the software can be transferred from one environment to another.

Process is a systematic and sequential set of activities to achieve a set of measurable goals.

A **program** is a type of recurring project such as the annual budget, not to be confused with a set of programming code.

Program Evaluation and Review Technique (PERT) was developed for the United States Department of Defense in the late 1950s. Specifically, it was developed by the consulting firm of Booz, Allen, and Hamilton for the U.S. Navy's Polaris submarine project (Polaris Weapon System). It combines statistics and network diagrams.

A **project** is an organized set of tasks to reach a measurable outcome within a specified duration.

The **Project Cost Updates** document updates initial project cost estimates at each major phase of implementation with comparison to the Initial Budget Estimate.

A **project's duration** is the total number of calendar days involved from start to end, including the project manager's activities in closing the project.

The **project manager** is the person with overall responsibility for managing and controlling the project tasks (defined and undefined) to achieve a measurable outcome within a specified schedule and budget.

The **Project Proposal** is a formal response to the Commercial Specification that describes the requirements for a project.

A **project schedule** is the duration (work-time plus the wait-time) of the project cycle.

The **Project Specification** is a formal response to the Commercial Specification that specifies the requirements for a project.

The **Project Support Plan** ensures that the project is supportable in a market environment. This plan should include a process for customer support.

A **project team** is an organization that is put together to achieve a specific set of measurable goals within a specific time and with limited resources, equipment, and materials.

Quality assurance is based on performance. It uses performance standards and benchmarks to determine the status of project goals.

A **quality audit** is an independent evaluation or test of some component of the project by qualified personnel.

Quality control is the component of quality management that considers the system or development processes of a project.

Quality management uses control and assurance to prevent risks and if a risk occurs to minimize it.

The **Quality Plan** defines the roles of quality control and assurance in all phases of the project process.

A **resource** is anything that supports the project. This includes, in general terms, money, skills, materials, time, facilities, and equipment.

Responsibility is the obligation or accountability given through assignment to complete a specific activity or task.

A **risk** is a performance error that can have a significant or disastrous impact on the success of a project or major activity. It is more than a problem; its effect can have an adverse or disastrous consequence on the project's outcome.

Role is a skill set with a label that perhaps explains the reasons for the actions and behavior of the actor.

Scalability is to what degree a network can be enhanced without a major change in design.

> At the fictional Internet company depicted in the commercial mentioned earlier, **scalability** was not adequately addressed. An Internet project **scope plan** would have to focus on key issues, such as load-time or hosting.

The **Schedule** is the duration of the project, including production-time and wait-time. It is also a production plan for the allocation of tasks with deadlines.

Scope is the amount of work and resources (skills, materials, and equipment) required for project completion.

Scope defining is extending the measurable goals to become general procedures with measurable constraints and viable assumptions.

Scope planning is defining the project goals and the performance expectations of the goals in measurable terms, and getting agreement on them.

Skill level is a factor used by a project manager in planning the project's Budget, rather than using headcount.

Specific goals are project goals that are measurable, unambiguous, and match exactly the customer's stated expectations.

The **sponsor** is the one who provides the resources and the working environment to make possible the achievement of project goals.

A **stakeholder** is any person or organization interested in the project. This includes the customer, your boss, you, the team, and interested government regulators.

A **standard** is usually an external, industry-accepted document for achieving quality for one or more of the project-defined expected goals.

A **Statement of Work** (SOW) is an integrated set of descriptions as to project tasks, goals, risks, and resources to complete a measurable outcome.

A **strategic manager** heads an area of a corporation that includes the IS project as a part of that person's performance goals.

The **tactical manager** is the one responsible for the overall flow of the project process so that the strategic goals are met.

A **task** is a cohesive work unit that is meaningful for tracking that is a set of activities. Writing a line of code is not a task, but writing a module that handles a specific function is a task.

A **team** is a group with a common purpose and with skills that compliment each other.

The **Third-Party Market Agreement** provides the plans whereby the entire project or a part of the project is to be the responsibility of a third-party developer.

The **Third-Party Service Plan** defines how the project is to be serviced by a third-party developer.

A **trade-off** is an act of balancing project constraints.

The **Training Strategy** shows how training is to be designed, developed, implemented, and verified.

The **Trial (Beta) Strategy** identifies the software and hardware elements in the project that are a part of any trial. The "where," the "when," and the "whom" should be included in the strategy. This provides a clear identification of the testing requirements plus the extent of the resources and capabilities necessary to trial.

Variance is any deviation from the planned work whether it is costs, time, or resources.

REFINING DATA BY ASKING THE CORRECT QUESTIONS

The common technique used throughout Section 1A of this book is the use of questions (interrogation) to determine data parameters, types of data parameters, assumptions, and constraints. Below are 20 examples of questions that might be used to refine any data types and associated data for a Scope Plan:

1. What are the customer's calculable goals and deliverables?

Goals and deliverables are data types. The actual customer goals and deliverables are the data. A response to this question should not be open to interpretation. This is a firewall to resolve customer expectations.

2. How will the goals be funded and budgeted?

Remember from the discussion on project viability: If there is no funding, there is no project. Is the funding in weekly, monthly, or quarterly increments? A project's funds should never be a single budget item. Remember the obvious: Your departmental budget is revisited perhaps at the end of each quarter. A project budget is not a corporate budget!

3. What are the critical tasks for achieving the critical goals?

An essential component of any scope plan is a critical path. A critical path is the minimum number of tasks that can be achieved in the least amount of time to reach the defined, measurable goals that are necessary, not optional or nice. Based on the project's objectives a critical path includes these data types: critical tasks, resources, cost and time estimates; requirements for skills, training, and documentation; and justifications.

4. What resources are critical for success?

Critical resources are the minimal required tasks and resources as defined in a pessimistic scenario.

5. What are the criteria for defining pessimistic, realistic, and optimistic estimates?

These criteria need to be based on objective sources and must be defined prior to writing estimates. The earliest, modern project-management program, PERT, used as a criterion a one-in-twenty scenario that an event would or would not happen.

6. Have potential threats and opportunities been identified for schedule changes?

A threat is not necessarily a risk. A risk produces project failure. An opportunity might be used to reduce a project's duration or funding.

7. What tasks or expected goals require training?

Training includes hands-on learning curves. Neglecting to define the informal training may cause a bigger risk than the formal training events.

8. Wh at are the criteria for documenting the project tasks?

The project team with input from the customer should define up front what tasks must be documented. Because of project goals documentation requirements should be considered in the same manner as the training requirements. Any document on a software application or utility should not be written without input from the programmers.

9. How should the project's scope definition be used to develop the Schedule?

The Scope Plan should include event durations, milestones, and so forth; these should be used to create the Schedule. Usually a schedule is a formal statement of tasks within a calendar structure with links to goals.

10. Where have delays been factored into the Schedule?

Factored potential delays are contingencies, not padding. Delays come in the standard scenarios. This means you have three schedules that reflect these scenarios.

11. How do cost estimates affect the schedule?

A cost estimate may generate a budget item. When funding will be available does affect the schedule. In a start-end schedule situation, you may need to have the funding in the Budget prior to the beginning of the task, such as payment to a consulting firm.

12. How do resource estimates affect the Schedule?

A resource estimate may generate a budget item. When the resource will be available does affect the Schedule. For example, however, you may need a special piece of hardware before a task can start, such as a tester to be use by quality assurance.

13. Are there any internal or external procurement policies or standards that affect the schedule?

More project managers are caught on not being aware of the impact of procurement policies than on any other policy data type. Do you, as the project manager, have the authority to procure capital resources?

14. How is training to be accomplished?

Training may be internal, external, hands-on, formal, or informal. There might be online courses, classroom experiences, text, or seminars. In all cases, you need to consider learning curve impacts.

15. How is documentation to be accomplished?

Documentation can be by a corporate writing group, by IS technical personnel, or purchased out-of-the-box.

16. Who is to create the organizational structure that links responsibilities tasks and deliverables?

The "who" of this question may be a team rather than an individual.

17. What are the standards and benchmarks for the quality assurance and control program?

There must be identified standards and benchmarks for any quality management program. The standards can be both external (organizations or companies) and internal (corporate, IS, or project team developed).

18. What are performance criteria for the quality assurance program?

Quality assurance's performance criteria should be based on objective criteria from the standards and benchmarks collected in response to question 17. An IS department probably has more usability data than any other corporate group. These data are gathered because of the need to know about network usage and users.

19. What is the necessary time for quality validation?

Validation should be defined at the beginning of the project, not as an afterthought. Validation is an internal check, while testing is a field situation check.

20. Who should be involved in a customer review?

The response may be more an emotional one than a rational one. Begin by defining what the project team means by a customer review. Some people think customers should not be at a customer review.

Remember any of the above questions can be rewritten to reflect any of the metaquestions. Using the last question as an example:

- How should you manage a customer review?
- Why should there be a customer review?
- When should you hold a customer review?
- Where should you hold a customer review?
- What are the assumptions and constraints for holding a customer review?

Another set of questions beyond these 20 should be determined by the local situation; that is, questions on the technological situation. The interrogative set begins with "Why should any piece of hardware or software application be used for this project?"

USING THE FORM AND CHECKLIST PROCESS

The Scope Plan is not only the project's assumptions and constraints, but it is also the framework or foundation for the whole project. It is a living document by adding as appendices the other project management documents such as the Schedule and the Budget.

The Scope Plan is the actual of the potential of the project viability survey. You can use the Checklist for Project Viability Questions (01viable) as the framework or structure for creating data types for forms for the Scope Plan. The following is an example document structure for the data and data types used in the management process of a project:

1. Scope definition

This is the opening section of the Scope Plan that includes the measurable project goals and deliverables.

2. Project assumptions and constraints

Whenever applicable, there should be assumptions and constraints for each goal and deliverable. This may be your first real evaluation of potential risk areas.

3. Authority statement

There must be a clearly written statement from the funding authorities that you, the project manager, have the function to decide the legal response to all situations. This does not mean the project manager should be involved in minutia, but in the critical direction and results of the project.

4. Organizational structure with responsibility links

As much as the "tree" organizational structure or hierarchy is endured in corporate life, a project's organizational structure must reflect the working reality that people are grouped by common responsibilities, even across defined corporate functional groups.

5. Baseline plan

This plan includes performance deviations, and the bibliography and location of all technical and quality benchmarks and standards.

6. Estimate criteria

You need three types of estimates — pessimistic, realistic, and optimistic. The estimates must consider:

- Resources (hardware, software, materials, and skills)(Chapter 4A)
- Time (Chapter 5A)
- Cost (Chapter 7A)
- Risk levels (Chapter 10A)

7. Communication program

This program gives the "who" that gets the "what," "when," and "how." The "where" is implied with the "who." You should define the criteria that give you the most effective and efficient forms of communications for all appropriate circumstances.

8. Risk management parameters

These parameters include unacceptable risk criteria, confidence level, correction process or framework, and review process. This area is discussed in more detail in Chapter 10A.

9. Training program

You need a program to train your personnel in the skills required to achieve the tasks. In addition, you may need a training program for one or more of the project deliverables.

10. Documentation program

Besides the documentation plan, you might include the following project documents as appendices to the Scope Plan:

- Budget, with Contingency Items
- Business Affiliate Plan
- Business Justification
- Commercial Specification
- Content Agreement
- Customer Documentation Strategy
- Design and Development Plan
- Field Introduction Requirements
- Initial Budget Estimates
- Initial Funding Requirements
- Logistics Plan
- Market Analysis Report
- Project Proposal
- Project Specification
- Project Support Plan
- Quality Plan
- Schedule, with Contingency Statements
- Statement of Work

- Third-Party Market Agreement
- Third-Party Service Plan
- Training Plan
- Trial (Beta) Strategy

Although the above list is lengthy, it is not considered comprehensive or that all the documents are required in every situation.

When you have an appropriate outline for your Scope Plan, it becomes a management tool. An effective management tool uses an organized data type and data questionnaire or survey that results in comprehensive measurable goals with valid assumptions and constraints. Including the various project documents requires that you ensure data consistency in the body of the Scope Plan with its support documents. Noting the support documents up front causes the project team to consider data requirements that, if determined later might have a negative effect on the project being on schedule and on budget.

The form and instructions in Chapter 28A are examples only. You should answer "Not applicable" on the form when a response is not required. This response gives you a historical record that item was considered.

02Scopef — Data Type/Data Refinement for a Scope Plan

02Scopei — Instructions for Scope Refinement Form

Chapter 3A

Creating and Managing an Activity Plan

OBJECTIVES: At the end of this chapter, you will be able to:

- Recognize the benefits and consequences for having a procedure for task identification.

- Identify 78 concepts that are relevant in developing a set of questions used to create an activity plan.

- Develop the skill to use an interrogative process for creating or enhancing the Activity Plan.

- Become aware of how to develop an outline form or checklist that can refine and enhance the Activity Plan.

The tasks for developing a schedule and related forms and checklists are discussed in Chapter 6A.

Consider the real-life case of a software startup company with limited resources, in which the head of development also functioned as the creative director. That meant that the company's first product would be the design of one person with almost unlimited authority and no one to answer to. When the first build of the technologically sophisticated product was complete, the potential clients who were interested in the application were very unhappy with the look and feel of the user interface.

Because there had been no design phase written into the development (activity) plans, there was never adequate critique of the user interface even at the internal level. This lack of planning lengthened development time because a new user interface — with more intuitive navigation and more commercial visual design — had to be designed.

In other words, the Activity Plan must include all aspects in the development of a project, including the design implementation phases if applicable.

CREATING A TASK IDENTIFICATION CHECKLIST

A major project document is the Activity Plan, which really is a Task Plan. A task is a group of activities. An activity is the smallest management unit for the day-to-day operational area. The Activity Plan, contrary to its title, should not be bogged down in the minutiae of operational activities, but unfortunately this does happen.

You need to use a formal process of reviewing the tasks and their sequences to meet the project measurable goal. You build your cost, time, resource, and skill estimates with durable concrete rather than with adobe, which might come apart in a heavy rain.

A standard statement about project failure is that failure is probably caused by "bad" cost or time estimates. One worker in an interview said that he had worked on four projects and three of them failed. He stated the projects failed because of "poor" estimates.

If one identifies failure based on "poor" cost and time estimates, then one must also identify the reasons for the "poor" estimates. If you justify each of your project tasks, your involvement in the project will not be a reason for failure.

A project can fail because a person in upper management might arbitrarily decide that it might make the manager look good to cut funding to the project, thus causing project failure. You may be angry, but at least you can look yourself in the mirror and know you were professional in handling your project responsibilities.

In the current economic climate, many projects are being terminated even in apparently healthy companies as a means of cutting costs. Other projects that are in full swing may suffer resource or budget cutbacks. In these circumstances, project managers must remain flexible, able to rethink scope, and, if necessary, oversee the redesign and retasking of a project.

USING ESSENTIAL TERMS

While there are a number of terms important to this discussion, 11 terms are essential:

An **activity** at the operational level (a task at the tactical level) is the effort required to achieve a measurable result that uses time and resources.

An **event** is a point in time such as the start or end of an activity or task.

A **task** is a cohesive work unit that is meaningful for tracking that is a set of activities. Writing a line of code is not a task, but writing a module that handles a specific function is a task. A task is a set of activities.

A **deliverable** is a clearly defined project result, product, or service.

A **milestone** is a clearly defined date of start or date of 100% completion of a set of tasks.

A **gate** is another term for milestone or a major project event.

The **Activity Plan** is a set of definitions that includes the task constraints from the Scope Plan.

Activity planning is documenting a plan that establishes constraints and assumptions for any tasks taken during the project process.

Activity sequencing is the determination of a logical order of activities or tasks that are used in developing a realistic and achievable schedule.

A **constraint** is a parameter, limitation, or a boundary for the project plan such as the Budget or the Schedule.

An **assumption** is a prediction that something will be true, either a task or an event that ensures project success such as, "There will be identified potential risks, but they will be overcome."

ADDING SUPPORTIVE TERMS

Besides the 11 essential concepts given above, an additional 67 terms, concepts, and document definitions are given below. You also need to consider the discussions given in Chapters 1A and 2A in developing the Activity Plan. For example, you need to note in the Activity Plan the general tasks for writing and publishing documents discussed in the earlier chapters in the context of the concepts discussed in this chapter.

Ability is the capacity to achieve or to perform; it is enhanced through training

An **audit** is a formal study of the project as a whole, or a project's component, as to status (progress and results), costs, and procedures.

A **benchmark** is a specific technical level of excellence.

Budgeting is entering cost estimates into a formal financial structure.

A **checklist** is an organized list, possibly a standard of action, that usually has to be followed in sequence to accomplish a specified goal.

Communication is oral or written transfer of data or information between individuals.

Communications is the process of getting the correct data to the correct person at the correct time in a cost-effective manner.

A **consultant** is a person from outside the normal resource pool with experience in solving a specific project issue.

Control is the monitoring of progress and the checking for variances in the plan.

Cost estimating is the process of establishing or defining the amount to be budgeted for a task based on constraints and assumptions from the project goals for the duration of the task, the average skills required for completing the task, and the resources required for completing the task.

A **critical activity** or task if not completed means project failure.

A **critical path** is when there is no available time for the slippage of the activity or task (no slack time).

The **critical path method** (CPM), in its simplest form, is selecting the "must" activities or tasks, and doing them in the shortest possible amount of time and within the shortest duration. CPM is a network diagramming technique and can be used to estimate the project's earliest completion by establishing the longest series of activities or tasks.

Duration is the total involved time of an activity or a task, including production-time and wait-time.

Effectiveness is the attained measure of quality to complete the activity, task, or event. It is also the skill required to define goals and to accomplish them.

Efficiency is the measurement of output based on amount of input. It is also the skill that can accomplish maximum output with minimum input.

The **end-end dependency** means that an activity or task cannot end until another one has also ended.

The **end-start dependency** means that an activity or task must end before another one can start.

An **estimate** is a guess based on opinion, or a forecast based on experience. Cost, time, and resource estimates are the foundations for project planning.

Expectation is a stated project goal that can become a perceived undocumented result.

Feedback is an activity of the personnel evaluation process task that should be held on a regular basis in which the status of the person being evaluated can be clearly stated based on measurable standards or benchmarks.

A **Gantt chart** is a visual presentation, using a horizontal bar chart and that shows activities or tasks against time. It is named after its developer, Henry Laurence Gantt.

Goal characteristics have to be measurable, specific, and potentially possible.

Headcount is a factor used by business managers in planning an annual budget, but should not be used by project managers.

The **Initial Budget Estimates** provides a view of the expected development costs, which are usually based on the estimates in the Preliminary Project Specification. This document is updated in the Project Cost Update.

The **Initial Funding Requirements** document is for monitoring and reporting project costs at each major phase of the project. It should include comparisons to the original funding document used to establish financial targets and expected milestones and deliverables.

Interoperability is the degree to which the various network components work with each other successfully.

Lag-time is the time between two activities or tasks because of their natures.

Lead-time is the overlapping time of two activities or tasks.

A **learning curve** is a graphical representation of repetitive tasks that when done on a continuous basis lead to a reduction in activity duration, resources, and costs.

Leveling is the technique to smooth out peaks and valleys in the use of resources.

Logistics is the process of getting the correct resource to the correct location at the correct time.

The **Market Analysis Report** documents and verifies market opportunities and justifies the features, services, and applications for the project goals.

A **model** is a theoretical environment with as much data as possible to reflect reality adequately for decision-making.

A **node** is a network event that is achieved or is not achieved. A milestone is a node type.

An **objective** is a set of measurable goals to achieve a defined target, that if not achieved, has critical results.

An **operational manager** is the person that handles the day-to-day operations or activities for a specific functional group or area that has been defined in the project plan.

An **opportunity** is a situation that will positively affect the project in time, money, resources, or all three in a significant manner.

An **optimistic estimate** is an assumption that holds that everything will go as planned.

An **organization chart** is normally a visual representation of who reports to whom. It shows the hierarchical and perhaps functional relationships among organizational groups. The project organization chart must include the core project responsibilities of each team member.

Padding is an informal action, such as adding time or cost to an estimate, that should not happen. These estimates should be formalized in a contingency plan.

A **path** is a sequence of lines within a network diagram in which the most important is labeled critical. The critical path is the timeline of the necessary work to be completed in the minimum amount of time.

Performance is the measurable level of action to achieve a measurable project goal. It is the act or level of work demonstrated and judged based on identified skill level.

A **pessimistic estimate** is the assumption that if something can go wrong, it will.

A **phase** is a project segment such as planning, designing, and developing.

Portability is a characteristic of software. It is the degree to which the software can be transferred from one environment to another.

Process is a systematic and sequential set of activities (tasks) to achieve a set of measurable goals.

A **project** is an organized set of tasks to reach a measurable outcome within a specified duration.

A **project's duration** is the total number of calendar days involved from start to end, including the project manager's tasks in closing the project.

A **quality audit** is an independent evaluation or test of some component of the project by qualified personnel.

The **Quality Plan** defines the roles of quality control and assurance in all phases of the project process.

A **realistic estimate** is an assumption that there will probably be a few difficulties, but with compromise, the difficulties will be overcome.

A **resource** is anything that supports the project. This includes, in general terms, money, skills, materials, time, facilities, and equipment.

> When putting together the Activity Plan, it is an excellent idea to find a way to keep track of human resources, especially when people are pulled off one project and put on another. You might consider creating a resource tracker that could be easily accessed on a special drive in the network or on a company intranet.

Resource planning is establishing support requirements for a project as to costs, availability, start-date and end-date (length of time for use plus duration), and technical specifications.

A **risk** is a performance error that can have a significant or disastrous impact on the success of a project or major task. It is more than a problem; its effect can have an adverse or disastrous consequence on the project's outcome.

Scalability is to what degree a network can be enhanced without a major change in design.

Scheduling is the task that formalizes the time estimates within a calendar structure. It is an integration of sequencing tasks, resource planning, cost estimating, and time estimating.

Skill level is a factor used by a project manager in planning the project's Budget rather than using headcount.

Slack time is the difference between earliest and latest (start or finish) times for an activity, a task, or an event.

Slippage (budget) is when a budget item is overspent.

Slippage (time) is expected when you know about it before the due date. It is unexpected when you learn about it after the fact that is after the due date.

Specific goals are project goals that are measurable, unambiguous, and match exactly the customer's stated expectations.

A **standard** is usually an external industry-accepted document for achieving quality for one or more of the project-defined expected goals.

The **start-end dependency** means that an activity or a task must begin before another one can end.

The **start-start dependency** means that one activity or task must start before another.

The **state-change model** is concerned with conditions and events that can change the state of your enterprise network.

A **Statement of Work** (SOW) is an integrated set of descriptions as to project tasks, goals, risks, and resources to complete a measurable outcome.

Time estimating is concerned with the duration of an individual activity or groups of related activities (tasks).

A **trade-off** is an act of balancing project constraints.

REFINING DATA BY ASKING THE CORRECT QUESTIONS

Before discussing a refinement process, you must clearly comprehend the 11 essential terms or concepts given at the beginning of this chapter. Following is a simple relationship structure:

- An *activity* is an *event* with a start- and finish-date that uses resources, such as designing a section of an application. An activity is primarily operational datum.
- A *task* is a collection of activities, such as designing all the sections of an application. A task is a data type.
- A *deliverable* is a designed application or product.
- A *milestone* or *gate* is the actual start- and finish-dates of the designing task for the application or product.
- The management process for handling activities is called *activity planning* and *sequencing*, and the process is documented in the *Activity Plan*.
- The rational basis for how, why, when, where, who, and what is defined by the *assumptions* and *constraints* as documented in the Activity Plan. Thus, an assumption or a constraint can have up to six basic components.

It may be unsatisfactory to state that a constraint of a section of application will be written in less than 100 lines of code. You may have to explain why this constraint is necessary.

The ten questions that follow should assist you in either structuring your Activity Plan or in identifying any omissions in the plan. Remember, the Activity Plan is not only the plan for operational tasks, but also the constraints and assumptions for performing the operational tasks. The following questions do not require responses that are data oriented, but that are procedural oriented.

1. Have criteria for estimating (cost, time, and resources) been defined?

You need objective criteria for project estimates. The essential sources are standards and benchmarks. There need to be of a consistent type for the estimates.

2. Have criteria for defining a critical task been created?

A critical task should be defined only when there is objective support, such as the need for a design phase for a new piece of hardware or software. This point may appear to be obvious, but on occasion, especially in large companies with an enormous amount of software, there is a tendency to do a cut-and-paste without design considerations to the new whole.

3. Have criteria for strategic, tactical, and operational activities been created?

Such criteria need to define the policy activities, the project administrative activities, and the work activities. An example: an operational manager does not discuss about making changes with a customer in private. Any change needs to go through the project manager and must be documented. What does this mean? It means that here must be a change mechanism, defined with its appropriate activities.

4. What is the impact of the availability of resources on the Activity Plan?

The activities that are required for resource availability need to be defined. One area of activities that is often omitted is procurement; when omitted, it causes a major bottleneck. Any procurement group has rules, forms, and procedures for the acquisition of hardware from the inexpensive to the expensive. There needs to be a set of activities or procedures for any capital expenditure as part of the up-front (planning) process for a project.

5. How can the Scope Plan be used to refine the Activity Plan?

The Scope Plan should define the assumptions and constraints for project tasks. The Scope Plan should support any set of tasks in the Activity Plan.

6. What are the criteria for writing the Activity Plan?

Later in this chapter, an outline for an activity plan is given. Each "chapter" or "appendix" should be considered a core data type. While criteria might be considered a data type, it is best to qualify them with such adjectives as skills or contingency. The point is more valid for the data type "estimate."

7. What are the documentation prerequisites for defining an activity or a task?

There needs to be some activities for project administrative documentation as well as documentation that might be used by the training and documentation groups. Too many of these groups have to determine their information gathering activities outside of stated project tasks.

8. When should the quality management procedures be stated in the Activity Plan?

This book is devoted to data form management because the tasks associated with it are not grouped as a data type, thus a quality management program lacks consistent data to establish valid baselines for tasks.

9. What are the criteria for risk management that may impact tasks?

Risks cause failure of the project. What activities need to be considered when the situation is worse than pessimistic? The data type is critical scenario tasks.

10. What are criteria for defining the training requirements for tasks?

There needs to be measurable project goals for the expectation of required training. A possible measurable goal could be "There are no requirements for training outside of necessary those to achieve specified project's goals." Do not become comfortable with this goal. Are hands-on experiences and the learning curve a part of training? In the Activity Plan in the chapter on training, this would be the first sentence and is a constraint on related training tasks. This sentence eliminates the data type of customer training or continuing training resulting from the creation of a product.

After resolving general procedural issues, you must consider the basic procedure that goes hand-in-hand with identifying tasks; that is sequencing each task's activities. Besides the word "sequencing," you could use "ordering" or "aligning." The first step in sequencing is to use the critical path method (CPM). All sequencing must resolve the critical tasks and their shortest timeline.

Do not confuse activity or task sequencing with scheduling. The Schedule includes the tasks and the amount of time that the task requires to be completed in a logically defined timetable, as well as the includes start and end dependencies and the lag and lead time relationships. You need to first decide the relationship of the product to the process status; that is, you must design a product before you develop it.

The questions that follow will assist in identifying holes in the activity sequences — each task might have its own sequence of activities. Would you sequence a configuring task before the installing task? In a project with 5000 activities or 125 tasks, one might actually make this mistake without a distinctive notation.

1. Why should the critical path method (CPM) be used for sequencing?
2. What are the criteria for identifying the sequence of activities?
3. How do the defined deliverables affect activity sequencing?
4. When does resource availability cause sequence collisions?
5. How does the budgetary cycle impact the project sequence?
6. How do documentation requirements impact the project sequence?
7. How does the training sequence link to the other, entire project sequences?
8. How do procurement policies relate to the project sequence?
9. Where do quality management procedures impact correct sequencing process?
10. What are the necessary links for the various sequence sets?

USING THE FORM AND CHECKLIST PROCESS

The structure (the data types) of your Activity Plan should be based on criteria developed using questions such as those given above. These criteria should also be used to determine your data types and data requirements. Thus, the first step in developing any form or checklist is to identify common and related groups of criteria. You must use one form for each task scenario. There may be functional differences, but you may have more data types in common than you might think. The Statement of Work is, of course, project type dependent.

The two important sets of data types are all of the task assumptions and task constraints. These probably will flow out of the project assumptions and constraints that were fully defined in the Project Plan.

Another step in developing data is to consider all the tasks needed for a deliverable, and then all the activities required for a given task. Next, you need do an analysis of what data are required by milestone or gate. At this point of activity sequencing, you would need to include the start- and end-dates.

Besides using the essential definitions, you must look also at the supportive definitions. An activity uses resources; that is money, time, skills, hardware, or software. This means you need estimates. One way to define resources is to label them critical, major, or minor; the most common way to define estimates is pessimistic, realistic (which is most likely), or optimistic.

In the Program Evaluation and Review Technique (PERT), an optimistic time improves only one-in-twenty, while pessimistic time in the negative of this ratio. Before doing any estimates you should decide the criteria for these each of three estimate types.

The Activity Plan becomes the foundation for the formal Schedule. Data requirements are determined by the corporate and project environments. The following is an example of a structure or chapters for an Activity Plan, which in turns implies types of data required:

1. Project goals and deliverables
2. Project assumptions and constraints
3. Criteria for estimates
4. Critical tasks and their critical activities

5. Skills criteria

6. Contingency criteria

7. Finance

8. Communications

9. Procurement

10. Quality management and verification

11. Training

12. Documentation

13. Risk management tasks

14. Appendices

- Contingency Plan
- Slippage Policy
- Market Analysis Report
- Initial Funding Requirements
- Initial Budget Estimates
- Quality Plan

Chapters 7 through 13 of this Activity Plan could have a separate section for each project phase such as design, development, testing, implementation, and verification.

The simplest form for any project activity is as follows:

Estimate	Optimistic	Realistic	Pessimistic
Cost	_____	_____	_____
Time	_____	_____	_____
Equipment	_____	_____	_____
Material	_____	_____	_____
Skill	_____	_____	_____

This form could be put on index cards and used in activity planning; the time estimates could be used to do activity or task sequencing. For a more complex application, you could put this framework in a spreadsheet and electronically tabulate data by categories.

The checklist in Chapter 28A reflects some of the data types required for possible chapters in the project Activity Plan. See the final ordered list in this chapter.

03actf — Task Identification Checklist

03acti — Instructions for Checklist for Task Identification

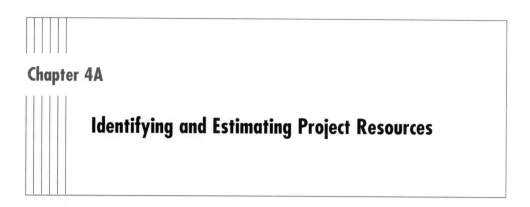

Chapter 4A

Identifying and Estimating Project Resources

OBJECTIVES: At the end of this chapter, you will be able to:

- Identify 37 concepts that are relevant to project resource form management.
- Develop the skill to use a query approach to determine resource data types.
- Learn to differentiate between headcount and skill count.
- Become aware of how to design and develop forms and checklists that can capture data for project resources.
- List ten ways to manipulate resource data.
- Identify 20 plus potential chapters and appendices for the Resource Plan.
- Identify a basic 9-step process for developing a resource plan checklist and instructions.

When it comes to selecting the people needed to complete a large-scale project, IS project managers often must decide whether to use outside resources such as consultants, or in-house talent. In the late 1990s the city of San Diego was involved in a Y2K remediation project, which its IS subsidiary could not handle because of the project's size and complexity, and a looming deadline. PricewaterhouseCoopers was brought in to hire off-shore manpower (Saytram in India), and oversee every aspect of the project. PricewaterhouseCoopers tracked the progress of the code remediation abroad and, as time grew short, suggested that the city's project managers communicate directly with the off-shore company to save time to meet the critical deadline. In this win-win situation, project managers from all points stayed in close contact in order to best manage extensive in-house and off-shore resources.

CREATING A RESOURCE PLAN CHECKLIST

The example form "Resource Plan Checklist" that is given in Chapter 28A is a "parent" form for resource management. You as the project manager must establish the assumptions and constraints for resource estimates. Resource estimates affect both cost and time estimates. A cost estimate may become invalid because of resource padding. A time estimate may become invalid because the resource's duration was estimated as too little or too much.

After this form is completed, specialized forms might be created to gather further data. However, an important instruction with this is "Attach additional information."

The keys to the form are two necessary actions:

- There must be three estimates for each resource: pessimistic, realistic, and optimistic.
- Each resource needs to be defined as critical, optional, or standard.

One of the most common mistakes in project management is only to have one estimate, whether it is cost, time, or resource. Each estimate must have a range, with the criteria for this range defined by the project before any resource definition. For example, in PERT a criterion was for example that an event would or would not happen once in 20 times.

In addition, by having three estimates, you minimize one of the most dangerous informal actions in any project, padding (unknown "protection"). Instead you need to move to a management position of having a known contingency. An obvious example of padding is the situation where a manager states the task needs four people rather than realistically two. An optimistic scenario might be one person, while a pessimistic might be four. Each scenario needs its own cost and time estimates.

When you have a set of forms that fulfill the second requirement, a sort can be done quickly to identify resources that have to be used in defining a critical path. A critical path is a document that gives the required activities (the critical resource list is a constraint) and the least amount of time (duration) to achieve a project goal.

In addition, when a resource is identified as critical, you need to know if it is available. A check mark indicating the unavailability of a resource is a flag for a potential risk. By knowing this, you can develop actions to eliminate this bump in the road.

Because there is a trend to use software to handle resource management, this form should give the data type information required to do the necessary input. It would be best to discuss the form with the software developer and to determine any additional information that can be defined. Likewise, if the reviewed software does not assist significantly in manipulation, look at other software applications. Do not buy a vendor resource management application without extensive review. One author wrote a 500 plus page on a well-known application. But was it the application that was needed?

When you use a management application, you will need, at a minimum the following information to ensure an adequate resource database:

- Identify calendar data.
- Identify cost (when and specific amount) of resources.
- Identify criticality of each resource.
- Identify links between resources.
- Identify links to tasks and people.
- Identify locations of resources.
- Identify physical amounts of each resource.
- Identify resource scenarios: pessimistic, realistic, and optimistic.
- Identify types of resources (hardware, software, skills, or materials)
- Identify usage of each resource.

The example checklist points directly and indirectly to these requirements.

USING ESSENTIAL DEFINITIONS

Any discussion in Section 1A also impacts this chapter; any discussion here must be filtered through these three fundamental concepts:

A **resource** is anything that supports the project. This includes, in general terms, money, skills, materials, time, facilities, and equipment.

Resource planning is establishing support requirements for a project as to costs, availability, start-date and end-date (length of time for use plus duration), and technical specifications.

An **estimate** is a guess based on opinion, or a forecast based on experience. Resource estimates are one foundation for project planning.

ADDING SUPPORTIVE DEFINITIONS

Besides the three essential concepts on resource planning given above you must also consider at least the following 34 definitions:

An **action plan** is the description of what is required to be completed and when it is to be completed.

The **Activity Plan** is a set of definitions for the efforts required to achieve measurable results. At the project level the efforts are tasks, while at the operational level they are activities and tasks.

An **assumption** is a prediction that something will be true, either an action or an event that ensures project success.

A **baseline plan** is the initial approved point from which any deviations will be determined using standards and benchmarks.

A **benchmark** is a specific technical level of excellence.

A **consultant** is a person from outside the normal resource pool with experience on solving a specific project issue. The consultant usually works from a biased position.

The **Content Agreement** is the written "contract" between the development group and the marketing group as to the content and functions of the project.

Contingency is the rational preparation for change.

A **contingency plan** is the preparation for a pessimistic scenario to become reality.

A regional hospital in New England initiated two large-scale clinical system (software) implementation projects. In both projects the budgets were guesstimates based on subjective criteria for risk. The greater the degree of uncertainty, the more likely would be later unforeseen costs. Because of their experience and knowledge, the in-house project team did an excellent job of identifying and preparing for contingencies, so the risk estimates in both projects later proved sound.

A **critical activity** or task if not completed means project failure.

Criticality is a position on the team where the individual in this situation has specific skills, usually technical, that if not available to the project, puts the entire project at risk.

Dependency means that a task has to be completed before a succeeding task can be completed.

Effectiveness is the attained measure of quality to complete an activity, task, or event. It is also the skill required to define goals and to accomplish them.

Efficiency is the measurement of output based on amount of input. It is also the skill that can accomplish maximum output with a minimum of input.

The **Field Introduction Requirements** document reflects the strategy and detailed plans to verify conformance to specification and functionality as defined in the Project Specification.

Headcount is a factor used by business managers in planning an annual budget but should not be used by project managers.

The **International Organization for Standardization** (ISO) is a consortium that sets standards in a variety of areas.

A **learning curve** is a graphical representation of repetitive tasks that, when done on a continuous basis, lead to a reduction in activity duration, resources, and costs.

Leveling is the technique used to smooth out peaks and valleys in the use of resources.

Logistics is the process of getting the correct resource to the correct location at the correct time.

A **management review** is a regularly scheduled performance review.

An **objective** is a set of measurable goals to achieve a defined target that, if not achieved has critical results.

An **optimistic estimate** is an assumption that holds that everything will go as planned.

Padding is an informal action, such as adding time or cost to an estimate, that should not take place. Any such estimates should be formalized in a contingency plan.

Performance is the measurable level of action to achieve a measurable project goal. It is the act or level of work demonstrated and judged based on identified skill level.

A **pessimistic estimate** is an assumption that if something can go wrong, it will.

The **Project Support Plan** ensures that the project is supportable in a market environment. This plan should include a process for customer support.

A **quality audit** is an independent evaluation or test of some component of the project by qualified personnel.

A **realistic estimate** is an assumption that there will probably be a few difficulties, but with compromise, the difficulties will be overcome.

Risk analysis is a technique, tool, or method for assessing either quantitatively or qualitatively (or both) the impacts of an identified risk or a potential risk identified through a scenario.

Skill level is a factor used by a project manager in planning the project's Budget, rather than using headcount.

A **standard** is usually an external, industry-accepted document for achieving quality for one or more of the project-defined expected goals.

The **Trial (Beta) Strategy** identifies the software and hardware elements in the project that are a part of any trial. Also the "where," the "when" and the "whom" should be included in the strategy. This provides a clear identification of the testing requirements plus the extent of the resources and capabilities necessary to trial.

Variance is any deviation from the planned work whether it is cost, time, or resources.

REFINING DATA BY ASKING THE CORRECT QUESTIONS

Because activities use resources, the data for the refinement of resources begins with the Activity Plan as discussed in Chapter 3A. The ten questions that follow should assist you in identifying your resources or in identifying omissions in the Resource Plan. Remember: The Resource Plan is not only for identifying resources for operational and administrative activities, but includes their utilization and availability constraints and assumptions.

Perhaps the biggest resource issue for you, as the project manager, is the need to recruit or allocate for skills rather than headcount. For business managers, headcount is a cardinal "bean counting" concept for establishing a budget. You can more easily define a salary for a head in a given organizational slot than try to determine salary by the head's skills. The assumption (and not a very good one) is that the ups-and-downs of the use of these skills should level out on an annual basis for any given individual; if not or a corporate reorganization is required. The consideration of skills versus headcount is important to project management because of the baseline goal of completing the project successfully on schedule and on budget.

The following 10 questions are used to answer the fundamental question of this step in the project management process: "What is the purpose of — why do we need of this resource?" These questions do not require responses that are specifically data (bits and bytes) oriented; they are purpose-oriented (hunks of data) so that they can assist you in identifying resource data types.

1. How can the Scope Plan be used to refine the Resource Plan?
2. How should measurable criteria for defining critical resources be created?
3. How should measurable criteria for estimating resources (emphasis on skills criteria) be defined?

4. How should measurable criteria for strategic, tactical, and operational resources be created to eliminate padding and create a source for contingencies?

5. What are measurable criteria for defining the training requirements (learning curve) for the use of resources?

6. What are the measurable criteria for writing the Resource Plan?

7. What are the measurable criteria for risk management that may impact resource acquisition?

8. What are the documentation prerequisites for defining and describing a resource?

9. What is the impact of the availability - having or not having - of resources on the project?

10. When should resource requirements be defined for the quality management procedures?

These questions as well as the following 10 must be answered in the context of your defined optimistic, realistic, and pessimistic measured goals for the project. Additionally, many of these questions can be changed to ask "why." For example, question 9 above could be restated as "Why should we be concerned with the availability of resource X?" You might say, "There is no concern."

Besides being concerned with the structure of the Resource Plan, you need to ask management questions that can help you focus on the decisions involving required skills and other resources necessary to achieve effective project goals:

1. How closely should resources been related to cost, time, and activity estimates?

2. How have the project scope definitions been used to plan resource estimates?

3. How do resources relate to each other?

4. What are the effects of the cost parameters on resource estimates?

5. What are the impacts of the milestones on the resource estimates?

6. What documents are required to control resources?

7. What are the ranges for having inadequate resources?

8. What is the control system to manage resources and any changes?

9. What procurement policies have to be followed?

10. Who defines the resource requirements?

The Resource Plan should be developed in concert with the Activity Plan (Chapter 3A). Thus, many of your resource questions will be the same as or similar to the ones developed for the Activity Plan. Both are baseline project documents; the guiding rule is simply that the activity or task needs to be defined before its resources.

WARNING: It is bad management to try to use an available resource to define activities for a project.

As discussed above, before you use the query process to determine resource data types and data, you must ask questions about structure of the Resource Plan and the management procedures for project resources. You need to test the water before you jump in.

EVALUATING RESOURCE DATA

A part of the form design process is to consider how you are going to manipulate the data. If you know how the data are to be manipulated, you can formulate an idea of the design resources forms and their instructions. Below are 10 possible ways you could manipulate resource data:

1. Make a list, as specific as possible, of required resources.

2. Identify mandatory resources.

3. Identify resources as belonging either to a pessimistic, an optimistic, or a realistic scenario.

4. Identify resources that belong to a contingency plan (based on a pessimistic scenario).

5. Group resources by project phase: planning, designing, developing, testing, or implementing.

6. Order the resources by priority — you need to first define what you mean by priority.

7. Group resources by users, this can be by organization or by individual.

8. Group resources by impact; that is as mandatory or optional such as the resource has to be available before starting activity or task X.

9. Group resources by availability — full-time, part-time, purchase, rent, and so forth.

10. List resources by training requirements.

From this list, you should see that a set of instructions required for filling out a form correctly and appropriately is critical to resource management. You have a block or space on a form labeled as "Resource Description," but in the instructions, you need to tell the user to include, if possible, the following data in the description:

- Mandatory or optional
- User — the organization or if one user, the individual's name and location
- When to be used
- Availability
- Cost in dollars and time
- If it is a contingency resource
- Time requirements — just for one day or through the entire design phase
- Training requirements for the resource (this is required when describing skills)
- If the resource based on a pessimistic, optimistic, or realistic view of achieving project goals
- Where the resource is to be used

One officer of a brick and mortar enterprise takes a more old-fashioned approach. He insists that all new projects come from in-house initiators with highly accurate estimates based on the lowest possible cost and time, and contrasted with the highest possible cost and time investments. He then asks three critical questions, which the project managers must be able to answer up-front: (1) How much business value depends on the project? (2) What could go wrong? (3) What will the project managers do if someone essential to the project's success quits?

COLLECTING DESCRIPTIVE, PRESCRIPTIVE, AND MANIPULATIVE DATA

Before designing a form for collecting data concerning resources, you need to identify, at the very least, these four data types:

- Criteria
- Skills
- Equipment (hardware and software)
- Materials

Underpinning all four data types is the need for valid time and cost estimates.

All criteria and skills should be measurable. You would not have a resource skill definition as simple as "An XML programmer is required." You must include the measurable deliverables from the programmer to achieve a specific project goal. You certainly need this information if you have to procure an outside consultant. Likewise, you do not say "The project requires a firewall." You need to specify the security, technical functions, standards, and benchmarks required as a basic resource description. Estimates for cost and time should be given against the following five data types:

1. Resource descriptions
2. Links
3. Impacts

4. Usage criteria

5. Change requirements

> For all five data types, you must ask the metaquestions. For each resource you must know:

- Why (purpose) is the resource needed?
- How (method) is the resource going to be used?
- Who (single user or multiple users) is going to use the resource?
- Where (location) is the resource going to be used?
- When (production and wait times and duration) is the resource to be used (one time, more than once or on a continuous basis)?

Beyond these basic minimum sections, the Resource Plan might also include these chapters:

1. Project goals and deliverables

2. Project assumptions and constraints

3. Criteria for estimates

4. Criteria for resource approval and acquisition

5. Critical resources

6. Skills criteria

7. Contingency criteria

8. Links to goals, deliverables, and tasks

9. Finance

10. Communication

11. Procurement

12. Training

13. Impacts for unavailable resources

14. Risk management

15. Appendices

- Contingency Plan
- Resource Management Policy
- Resource Utilization Policy
- Resource Change Management Policy
- Content Agreement
- Field Introduction Requirements

The Resource Plan is where you state the descriptive data (goals), the prescriptive data (criteria), and manipulated data (list of mandatory resources). The forms are used for collecting unprocessed resource data; that is, data values.

> The simple form given at the end of Chapter 3A could also be used for any resource.

USING THE FORM AND CHECKLIST DESIGN PROCESS

Remember: The technological environment significantly affects your local design form and checklist requirements. Your local technical requirements shape the instructions, because you may want to clearly define your instructional requirements under different scenarios. In addition, you might read external IS or IT standards found on the Internet that are related to the project's resource requirements.

The steps for the design and development of the checklist were done in parallel with its instructions. The checklist was edited or revised from its original draft because of the need for a logical flow to the instructions or the data capture process.

- The first step is to sketch out the administrative data required (that is, the name of person filling out the checklist, the date, the organization, and so forth).
- The second step is to sketch out the data capture requirements. For example, you could use the method given earlier in this chapter for "Resource Description."

- The third step is to draft the instructions.
- The fourth step is to revise the instructions for logical flow and completeness.
- The fifth step is to revise the checklist based on your latest set of instructions.
- The sixth step is to have the checklist and instructions reviewed by the appropriate project team members to ensure that all required data to be captured for a given type of resource are stated.
- The seventh step is to test the checklist and the instructions with several users to see if they can fill out the checklist appropriately.
- The eighth step is to make any required revisions.
- The ninth and final step is to implement the checklist.

In Chapter 28A is an example checklist with instructions that can be used for determining potential resource data types based on the structure for your Resource Plan.

04resf — Checklist for Defining Resource Data Types

04resi — Instructions for Using the Checklist

Chapter 5A

Creating Manageable Time Estimates

OBJECTIVES: At the end of this chapter, you will be able to:

- State a rationale for using a time estimate checklist.
- Identify 43 concepts that are used to develop a set of questions to refine your time estimates.
- Develop the skill to use an interrogative process to establish reliable time estimates.
- Learn to differentiate between a set of time estimates and a schedule.
- Become aware of how to develop a checklist used to enhance time estimates.

There are basically two ways to create and schedule time estimates on a project. One is to be given a deadline – originating with upper management, clients, or elsewhere — by which the project must be delivered. This requires real-time, end-goal planning. The other is to set estimates and produce a plan that all invested parties agree on. This is called open planning. Although open planning sounds ideal, it is far too easy to let timelines (and budgets) creep, unless you have the luxury of working in a blue-sky R&D department.

In reality, most project managers will work with time definitions of some sort, so time estimates must be calculated wisely. Bear in mind the project manager who saw that the system upgrade project that was being lead would not be completed on time, so the testing phase was cut short. The operational manager noticed the short cuts (risk) that were being taken, forced the weighing of two factors against each other: The risk of missing the deadline resulting in customer dissatisfaction versus the risk that of bringing up a system that could have problems that adequate testing would have revealed. The decision to push the deadline back was eventually made by the management team that oversaw the project, not by the project manager acting alone.

USING A TIME ESTIMATE CHECKLIST

One of the major reasons for project failure is having too many shoddy time estimates. You need to use a time estimate checklist as rigorous as an airplane pilot's takeoff checklist. When you do not do this, you are opening the door for time estimates to generate a risk, which will grab a well-known part of your anatomy.

The time estimate checklist ensures that you consider the three scenarios: pessimistic, realistic, and optimistic. The traditional method of doing a time estimate is having only one that probably has been padded. By having three estimates, you can develop an effective contingency plan, identify potential risk areas (a breakdown of a pessimistic scenario), and manage the project based on a critical path baseline.

WARNING: The Schedule is a project management tool used to make status presentations to the customer and to upper management. When the Schedule has too many shoddy time estimates, you are putting yourself in a very embarrassing position to say the least.

What are the chances that an IT development project will come in on time and under budget? Pretty unlikely, according to some industry analysts. In 1998, over half of all projects came in late and over budget and only about 16% were completed on schedule.

USING ESSENTIAL DEFINITIONS

You need to recognize that any discussion on estimates, — whether time, resource, or cost — is relevant to the discussion in this chapter.

However, the following five concepts are essential to any discussion about time estimates:

An **assumption** is a prediction that something will be true, either an action or an event that ensures project success.

A **critical path** is when there is no available time for the slippage of the activity or task (that is no slack time).

Duration is the total involved time for an activity or task, including production-time and wait-time.

An **estimate** is a guess based on opinion or a forecast based on experience. One of the foundations for project planning is time estimating.

Time estimating is concerned with the duration of an individual activity or groups of related activities (tasks).

USING SUPPORTIVE DEFINITIONS

The following 38 concepts are used to refine the discussion of time estimates:

An **action plan** is the description of what is required to be completed and when it is to be completed.

The **Activity Plan** is a set of definitions for efforts required to achieve measurable results. At the project level the efforts are tasks, while at the operational level they are activities and tasks.

Activity sequencing is the determination of a logical order of activities or tasks that are used in developing a realistic and achievable schedule.

A **constraint** is a parameter, limitation or a boundary for the project plan such as the Budget or the Schedule.

Contingency is the rational preparation for change.

A **contingency plan** is the preparation for a pessimistic scenario to become reality.

A **critical activity** or task, if not completed, means project failure.

The **critical path method** (CPM) in its simplest form, is selecting the "must" activities or tasks, and doing them in the shortest possible amount of time, and within the shortest duration. CPM is a network diagramming technique, and can be used to estimate the project's earliest completion by establishing the longest series of tasks.

A **deliverable** is a clearly defined project result, product, or service.

Dependency means that a task has to be completed before a succeeding task can be completed.

The **Design and Development Plan** drives the project's Integration Plan that captures all major design and development deliverables and milestones for management tracking and reporting.

> When there is a time crunch, the design phase is often the first part of the project to be squeezed out. This could spell disaster, because the design phase charts the blueprint for project deliverables. In the case of product deliverables, the design specs will help quality management test better and more wisely, as well as ensure consistent quality.

The **end-start dependency** means that an activity or task must end before another can start.

An **event** is a point in time such as the start or end of an activity or task.

Lag-time is the time between two activities or tasks because of their natures.

Lead-time is the overlapping time of two activities or tasks.

A **learning curve** is a graphical representation of repetitive tasks that, when done on a continuous basis, lead to a reduction in activity duration, resources, and costs.

Logistics is the process of getting the correct resource to the correct location at the correct time.

A **management review** is a regularly scheduled performance review.

A **milestone** is a clearly defined date of start or date of 100% completion of a set of tasks.

An **objective** is a set of measurable goals to achieve a defined target that, if not achieved, has critical results.

An **optimistic estimate** is an assumption that holds that everything will go as planned.

Padding is an informal action, such as adding time or cost to an estimate, that should not take place. Any such estimates should be formalized in a contingency plan.

A **pessimistic estimate** is an assumption that if something can go wrong, it will.

A **project's duration** is the total number of calendar days involved from start to end, including the project manager's activities in closing the project.

A **quality audit** is an independent evaluation or test of some component of the project by qualified personnel.

A **realistic estimate** is an assumption that there will probably be a few difficulties, but with compromise, the difficulties will be overcome.

Resource planning is establishing support requirements for a project as to costs, availability, start-date and end-date (length of time for use plus duration), and technical specifications.

Risk analysis is a technique, tool, or method for assessing either quantitatively or qualitatively (or both) the impacts of an identified risk or a potential risk identified through a scenario.

The **Schedule** is the duration of the project, including production-time and wait-time. It is also a production plan for the allocation of tasks with deadlines.

Scheduling is the task that formalizes the time estimates within a calendar structure. It is an integration of sequencing tasks, resource planning, cost estimating, and time estimating.

The **Scope Plan** is the strategic view of the constraints and assumptions of the project as developed by the project team.

Slack time is the difference between earliest and latest (start or finish) times for an activity, a task or an event.

Slippage (time) is expected when you know about it before the due date, it is unexpected when you learn about after-the-fact, that is after the due date.

A **standard** is usually external, an industry-accepted document for achieving quality for one or more of the project-defined expected goals.

The **start-end dependency** means that an activity or task must begin before another can end.

The **start-start dependency** means that one activity or task must start before another.

A **trade-off** is an act of balancing project constraints.

Variance is any deviation from the planned work whether it is cost, time, or resources.

COMPARING TIME ESTIMATES TO THE SCHEDULE

The Schedule (Chapter 6A) is a formal document of the best set of time estimates that your project team was able to develop. However, the differences between the process of time estimating and scheduling are a bit more complex. Here are 10 comparisons between time estimating and scheduling:

1. Time estimates are durations of tasks, while a schedule is a formal plan.

> A task is a collection of activities. At the operational level, time estimates are by activities. At the project level, estimates are concerned with tasks.

2. Time estimates are inputs into project management software; scheduling is the automatic output.

3. Time estimating is a component of scheduling; scheduling is an integration of sequencing tasks, resource planning, cost estimating, and time estimating.

4. Time estimating is a consequence of analyzing; scheduling is a consequence of planning.

5. Time estimating is, at times, an art, while scheduling is, at times, a science.

6. Time estimating is concerned with an individual activity or with groups of related tasks, while scheduling is concerned with the complete project.

7. Time estimating is to the Schedule, as cost estimating is to the Budget.

8. Time estimating makes an educated guess about a given event, while scheduling is based on dependencies — the interrelationships of time, resources, and tasks.

9. Time estimating may be thought of as abstract, while scheduling may be thought as concrete.

10. The project manager and operational managers review time estimates, an upper level manager reviews the Schedule.

One may think scheduling is scientific (a common overstatement) because of available techniques and tools such as the Gantt chart. The scheduling output is only reliable as the time estimating inputs. The Gantt chart is an excellent visual presentation form, but it should not be equated to science, which fundamentally is the ability to repeat a measurement of an observable event.

> "Garbage in, garbage out" is more than a cliché. In this instance, it could read "Shoddy time estimates in, shoddy schedule out."

REFINING DATA BY ASKING THE CORRECT QUESTIONS

Along with bad cost estimates, bad time estimates can destroy a project more quickly than anything else. In fact, all risks are probably caused by inferior estimates (time, cost, or resource). For this reason, you must ensure that you have an excellent — not just good — interrogative process for refining your time estimates.

The responses to the following questions should be based on the goals and deliverables for your project and the tasks to achieve them. Think in terms of plus and minus; think in terms of an optimistic date and a pessimistic date, for both start- and end-dates, for an activity or a task. The completion point could be a range of days rather than a single day. You still need an absolute date (deadline) at the end of the range, but at least it is a "realistic" date.

> Unfortunately, an erroneous practice in time estimating is to give a duration of days without stating what the production- and wait-times are.

There are a number ways to develop questions on time estimates. The following 10 questions reflect the importance of impacts:

1. What are the impacts of resources on the time estimates?
2. What are the impacts of the quality control and assurance processes on time estimates?
3. What are the impacts of following procurement policies on time estimates?
4. How do changes in time estimates impact project results?
5. What is the financial impact of expanding or shortening a time estimate?
6. Where in the project do poor, critical time estimates impact success?
7. Whose inputs into the time estimating process make the most impact?
8. How does the project's duration impact the time estimating process?
9. When can time estimates be changed and cause the least impact on the project?
10. Why do headcount criteria rather than skill criteria have more impact on the project?

The fundamental baseline of time estimates should be the critical path. The level of an impact is evaluated from this measurement. The critical path method is the basic technique or tool for time estimates. The following 10 questions consider this technique for time estimate components.

1. What are the basic project assumptions and constraints that affect the time estimating process?
2. How should production-time and wait-time be noted in a time estimate?

3. When should time estimates be considered at both the activity and task levels?

4. What are the criteria for critical time estimates?

5. How should the time estimates be handled in the Scope Plan, Activity Plan, and Resource Plan?

6. Why is there a need for contingency time estimates?

7. Who approves time estimates?

8. What time dependencies have been considered in doing time estimates?

9. When is it important to consider lag- and lead-times in time estimates?

10. What are the criteria for defining a time estimate as optimistic, realistic, or pessimistic?

USING THE FORM AND CHECKLIST PROCESS

You can effectively and efficiently use the simple form given at the end of Chapter 3A as a jumping-off point for creating your own forms and checklists for time estimates. The reason for this is that time estimates are done in concert with activity planning and sequencing, and with resource planning.

There are a number of data types beyond the obvious pessimistic, realistic, and optimistic estimates. All the terms in following list are defined in the "Adding Supportive Definitions" section of this chapter:

- Duration
- Dependency
- End-start dependency
- Event
- Lag-time
- Lead-time
- Start-end dependency
- Start-start dependency
- Variant

In Chapter 28A there is an example checklist to assist you in the creation of adequate and reliable time estimates. Any form or checklist you create probably will be designed based on your responses to potential impacts to time estimates, the critical path method, criteria for time estimating, and the components defined above for time estimates.

05timef — Time Estimate Checklist

05timei — Instructions for Using a Time Checklist

Chapter 6A

Creating a Schedule

OBJECTIVES: At the end of this chapter, you will be able to:

- State how the differences between a Project Schedule and a company schedule can have benefits for a project manager.
- Identify 49 concepts that are relevant to the development of a set of questions used to polish the Schedule.
- Develop the skill to use an interrogative process to develop a reliable Schedule.
- Learn to distinguish between a schedule and a set of time estimates.
- Become aware of how to use a checklist that can enhance the design and development of a Project Schedule.

Before reading this chapter, you should read Chapter 4A on time estimates. Put most simply, "A schedule is a formal graphic document of a set of time estimates."

If you have been following the procedures outlined in this Supplement, then you have all the materials necessary to produce a schedule — the result of matching up planning with available resources. At this point, you might think that producing a schedule is just another onerous piece of paperwork, but its importance cannot be underestimated.

The Schedule is a graphic representation of time and resource estimates. It is the project plan that is presented to upper management and to clients. If you are working in a situation in which there is a lack of top management interest or communication, then the Schedule can help you facilitate buy-in and even collaboration. For the client, the Schedule functions as a road map for the project that might have seemed over-whelmingly complex before being evaluated, outlined, and illustrated.

In one case, an intranet for a small company had to be networked in a specific period of time. It would enable communication and collaboration among employees who regularly worked outside the office, as well as for those in-house who worked on projects together.

The systems administrator came up with a simple timetable of tasks and dates that eventually proved inadequate because it did not provide enough detail on activities and resources. The reports to other managers were vague – "running late" or "need a couple of days more." Because there was no concrete, visual measurement of time and tasks, the project ran over schedule.

Practically speaking, the Schedule helps you answer two funda-mental questions: Where *should* we be on the Schedule now? Where *are* we exactly?

USING A PROJECT SCHEDULE RATHER THAN A COMPANY SCHEDULE

A Project Schedule is not a company schedule! It is more comprehensive in its requirements. It should be graphic in format rather than just a set of data tables. It requires three scenarios for time estimates: pessimistic, realistic, and optimistic. It has links to resources, skills, and responsible people. It has a critical path. It is related to the Project Scope Plan. It is based on measurable goals. By using icons, you can identify essential events such as task- or project-phase deadlines. With these items plus the other items dis-cussed in this chapter you will need a checklist as given in Chapter 28A to ensure that you have a functional Project Schedule. With this document, you can manage on a daily basis and you have something you can show your customer and upper level management in status presentations.

WARNING: You may be saying, This is too much. I will just use a project management software application." Even if you do use project management software, the checklist should be used to develop the database requirements that have to be entered into the application to generate the Schedule. "Garbage in, garbage out" is very applicable with this document. All scheduling consequences come from how well you managed the de-velopment of your time estimates as discussed in Chapter 5A.

One constraint is that you might be required to adhere to a company policy on a schedule's format.

USING ESSENTIAL DEFINITIONS

Because a schedule is, first, a visual presentation of time-oriented efforts of a project and, second, a project standard or baseline for managing a project, there are a large number of essential concepts. Here are 14 essential concepts (the list actually could be longer):

The **Schedule** is the duration of the project, including production-time and wait-time. It is also a production plan for the allocation of tasks with deadlines.

A **critical activity** or task if not completed means project failure.

A **critical path** is when there is no available time for the slippage of the activity or task (that is no slack time).

The **critical path method** (CPM) in its simplest form is selecting the "must" activities, and doing them in the shortest possible amount of time, and within the shortest duration.

Duration is the total involved time of an activity or task, including production-time and wait-time.

The **end-start dependency** means that an activity or task must end before another can start.

An **estimate** is a guess based on opinion, or a forecast based on experience. Because a set of time estimates is the basis for any schedule, they are a foundation for project planning.

An **event** is a point in time such as the start or end of an activity or task.

Lag-time is the time between two activities or tasks because of their natures.

Lead-time is the overlapping time of two activities or tasks.

A **project's duration** is the total number of calendar days involved from start to end, including the project manager's activities in closing the project.

Scheduling is the task that formalizes the time estimates within a calendar structure. It is an integration of sequencing tasks, resource planning, cost estimating, and time estimating.

The **start-end dependency** means that an activity or task must begin before another can end.

The **start-start dependency** means that one activity or task must start before another.

> Critical-chain project management, which focuses on bottom-line results and reduced cycle time, is fast becoming standard practice for project managers. The critical-chain or critical-path method, when used in conjunction with computer-based collaboration tools, helps make quantitative risk management and effective scheduling possible.

USING SUPPORTIVE DEFINITIONS

One might think 14 concepts were enough for a discussion; however, here are an additional 35 concepts that are used in this discussion to refine the "schedule."

An **action plan** is the description of what is required to be completed and when it is to be completed.

The **Activity Plan** is a set of definitions for the efforts required to achieve measurable results.

Activity sequencing is the determination of a logical order of activities or tasks that are used in developing a realistic and achievable schedule.

An **assumption** is a prediction that something will be true, either an action or an event that ensures project success.

A **baseline plan** is the initial approved point from which any deviations will be determined using standards and benchmarks.

A **constraint** is a parameter, limitation, or a boundary for the project plan such as the Budget or the Schedule.

Contingency is the rational preparation for change.

A **contingency plan** is the preparation for a pessimistic scenario to become reality.

A **deliverable** is a clearly defined project result, product, or service.

Dependency means that a task has to be completed before a succeeding task can be completed.

The **Design and Development Plan** drives the project Integration Plan that captures all major design and development deliverables and milestones for management tracking and reporting.

A **Gantt chart** is a visual presentation using a horizontal bar chart, that shows activities or tasks against time. It is named after its developer, Henry Laurence Gantt.

A **gate** is another term for milestone or a major project event.

A **histogram** is the opposite of a Gantt chart because vertical bars are used to represent values.

A **learning curve** is a graphical representation of repetitive activities or tasks that, when done on a continuous basis, lead to a reduction in activity duration, resources, and costs.

Leveling is the technique used to smooth out peaks and valleys in the use of resources.

Logistics is the process of getting the correct resource to the correct location at the correct time.

A **management review** is a regularly scheduled performance review.

A **milestone** is a clearly defined date of start or date of 100% completion of a set of tasks.

An **objective** is a set of measurable goals to achieve a defined target if not achieved has critical results.

An **optimistic estimate** is an assumption that holds that everything will go as planned.

Padding is an informal action, such as adding time or cost to an estimate, that should not take place. Any such estimates should be formalized in a contingency plan.

A **pessimistic estimate** is an assumption that if something can go wrong, it will.

Process is a systematic and sequential set of activities (tasks) to achieve a set of measurable goals.

A **quality audit** is an independent evaluation or test of some component of the project by qualified personnel.

A **realistic estimate** is an assumption that there will probably be a few difficulties, but with compromise, the difficulties will be overcome.

Resource planning is establishing support requirements for a project as to costs, availability, start-date and end-date (length of time for use plus duration), and technical specifications.

Risk analysis is a technique, tool, or method for assessing either quantitatively or qualitatively (or both) the impacts of an identified risk or a potential risk identified through a scenario.

The **Scope Plan** is the strategic view of the constraints and assumptions of the project as developed by the project team.

Slack time is the difference between earliest and latest (start or finish) times for an activity, a task, or an event.

Slippage (time) is expected when you know about it before the due date; it is unexpected when you learn about it after-the-fact, that is after the due date.

A **standard** is usually external, an industry-accepted document for achieving quality for one or more of the project-defined expected goals.

Time estimating is concerned with the duration of an individual activity or groups of related activities (tasks).

A **trade-off** is an act of balancing project constraints.

Variance is any deviation from the planned work whether it is cost, time, or resources.

COMPARING A SCHEDULE TO TIME ESTIMATES

Just because you have a formal document does not make it realistic. Such a document is only as good as its inputs. Unfortunately, too many managers forget this principle when they look at the Schedule or the Budget such as those discussed in Chapter 8A. To comprehend the Schedule in the context of its inputs of time estimates, you must also be aware of how the process of scheduling compares to that of time estimating. The following 10 comparisons should give you some insight into the differences:

1. A schedule is a plan to follow, while time estimates are duration (production-time and wait-time) guesses for the completion of activities or tasks.

2. A schedule is primarily the concern of an upper level manager, while time estimates are the concerns of the project and operational managers.

3. A schedule is to time estimates as a budget is to cost estimates.

4. Scheduling is a consequence of planning; time estimating is a consequence of analyzing.

5. Scheduling is an integration of sequencing tasks, resource planning, cost estimating, and time estimating, thus time estimating is only one of a number of components of scheduling.

6. Scheduling is based on dependencies — the interrelationships of time estimating, resource defining, and activity describing.

7. Scheduling is concerned with the complete project, while time estimating is concerned with an individual activity or groups of related activities (tasks).

8. Scheduling is considered, at times, a science, while time estimating is usually considered a black art.

9. Scheduling is the automatic output from project management software, while time estimates are inputs.

10. Scheduling may be thought as a concrete process, while time estimating may be thought of as abstract process.

As is shown in the next two sections, the process of developing the Schedule is a complex process. When the Schedule is well done, more time is saved during the project's duration than the time spent in the original effort. The Schedule's logical structure and visual presentation, as well as the content, might make or break a project.

REFINING DATA BY ASKING THE CORRECT QUESTIONS

The core question for the design, development, and implementation of any schedule is "What is the most logical method of presenting integration tasks, based on reliable estimates and using a timeline, so that it communicates clearly the measurable project goals?" The following 10 questions as in prior chapters are based on the six metaquestions. This means that any question can have as many as six variations.

1. How will the budgetary procedures affect the Schedule?
2. How can resources be acquired on time?
3. How can the formulated schedule impact the outcome of project integration?
4. How were the scheduled, critical milestones determined to be realistic?
5. How will the Schedule and its changes be given to the customer?
6. What criteria have been used to define clearly the "who's," "what's," "where's," and "how's" and to place them in the Schedule?
7. What historical data are available to determine adequate resources?
8. When were the start- and end-times for expected deliverables identified?
9. Where in the Schedule are the events that require the appropriate people to approve the Schedule's status?
10. Why should you use visual information as the foundation of the format for the Schedule?

> The Schedule could be based on calendar time or on a critical path where the completion of a given event or set of events is important to completing the project goals.

As the project manager you should ask the following 20 questions about your tactical scheduling actions implied in each question is one or more data type requirements:

1. When applicable how are vendors to be given the schedule's status?
2. How can resources be available in accordance with the Schedule?
3. How can the company's budget cycle impact the Schedule, especially in the fourth quarter?

4. How do you ensure that the Schedule realistically reflects the training and documentation requirements?

5. How do varying cost estimates impact the Schedule?

6. How does the Schedule potentially impact the skills, resources, and materials required for the project?

7. How should resource leveling be used?

8. How was the Schedule developed using the project goals?

9. What are the criteria for ensuring that the quality management schedule is appropriate?

10. What are the project assumptions and constraints for developing the Schedule?

11. What are the risk criteria that can affect the Schedule?

12. What are the Schedule alignment criteria?

13. What lag and lead time relationships were defined?

14. What types of project management tools should be used to manage the scheduling process?

15. When should "forgotten" tasks be determined in the scheduling process?

16. When were estimates defined to average capabilities?

17. Where are the links in the Schedule for outside resources that are critical to the project's success?

18. Where in the Schedule are events that can be impacted by procurement policies?

19. Who defines the start- and end-time dependencies?

20. Why should issues be documented and discussed at meetings?

USING THE FORM AND CHECKLIST PROCESS

The development of any form or checklist must be based on the basic definition of a *schedule*; that is, it is the duration of the project, including production-time and wait-time. It is also a production plan for the allocation of tasks with deadlines. It is a formal, visual, logical, and chronological statement of time estimates for a project's tasks.

You need a schedule that is readable, usable, and reliable for the project team. The Schedule becomes one of the project fundamental documents used to give status presentations to your upper management and the customers. Perhaps the only forms or checklists you need that are related to a schedule are based on an analytical methodology for determining the basis for these status presentations. This basis can be a simple checklist that leads to complex input. The Schedule is a project baseline. You determine:

- What are the project variances.
- How the project variances occurred.
- When the project variances occurred.
- Where the project variances occurred.
- Why the project variances occurred.

Notice that "who caused the variances" is not listed. When you include this, you get into people issues, which can actually block the success of resolving the variances.

What data do you need? The data come from the Scope Plan, the Activity Plan, and the Resource Plan. A schedule is more that just a time line; a Gantt chart can be considered an example of a basic type of time line. Although the Schedule is a visual representation of the relationships of various task sequences, you also need supportive data. The most important task sequence is of course, the critical path. The critical path is derived from the critical tasks done in the least amount of time (that is no slippage).

From your time estimates, you should include support for their assumptions and constraints attached to the Schedule. Each activity should be given as duration with production- and wait-times, not just a dot on a calendar. The Schedule should be given in a 24X7 mode, because some of the logistic events may occur at any time. Essential technical data for tasks from the time estimates should include:

- End-start dependencies
- Lag time
- Lead time
- Start-end dependencies
- Start-start dependencies

You should develop links — especially to critical resources — using the data developed in Resource Plan. You need to have a clear notation as to the different types of links by using for example different colors or special icons as determined by the project team. (Do not use red and green because these two colors carry emotional burdens.) You need links indicating when critical skills, hardware, software, and materials are to be used.

In Chapters 7A and 8A, cost estimates and the Project Budget are discussed. There should be appropriate links for critical cost and budget data. For example, you might have links when funding is to occur, who is doing the funding, and how the funding is to be done.

There are three important data types from the Resource Plan that need to be linked to the Schedule. They are:

1. Who (single user or multiple users) is going to use the resource?
2. Where (location) is the resource going to be used?
3. When (production- and wait-times and duration) is the resource to be used (one time, more than once, or on a continuous basis)?

At the end of Chapter 3A is a simple form with an important implied idea. The idea is that, for any activity or task sequence. You should have three timelines: optimistic, realistic, and pessimistic. The basic use of this concept is for the critical path.

The ideas given here on data types associated with the Schedule are not considered inclusive. You must consider management abilities, the size of the project, the needs of your customers, the needs of your upper management, and, last but not the least, the abilities and needs of your project team.

The local situation ultimately determines the form of the Schedule. However, behind any list of data types, there is the assumption that you have reliable time estimates. (This issue was discussed in Chapter 5A.) The following is a short list of 10 data types you can use to refine or enhance a complete schedule:

1. Change notification schedule
2. Communications points schedule

3. Criteria for changing the schedule

4. Critical path with links to skills (who and where) and resources (user and location)

5. Quality control, assurance, and validation timeline

6. Schedule based on the Scope Plan, Activity Plan, and Resource Plan

7. Time allocated for risk management

8. Timeline (calendar or flow chart)

9. Timeline for acquiring skills, equipment, and materials

10. Timelines that are consistent and coherent

In Chapter 28A you will find the following:

06Schf — Checklist for Creating a Project Schedule

06Schi — Instructions for a Project Schedule Checklist

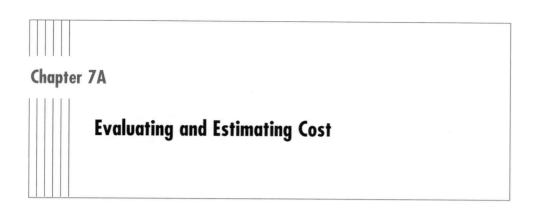

Chapter 7A

Evaluating and Estimating Cost

OBJECTIVES: At the end of this chapter, you will be able to:

- State a rationale for using a cost estimates checklist.
- Identify 43 concepts that are applicable to the development of a set of questions used to ensure reliable cost estimates.
- Develop the skill to use an interrogative process to refine cost estimates to achieve their reliability.
- Learn to discriminate between a set of costs and a budget item.
- Become aware of how to develop a checklist that can enhance final cost estimates that are reliable.

The legendary failures of many dotcom startups were captured in the recent documentary film *Startup.com*, which detailed the rise and fall of govWorks.com. The company's Web-based service enabled local governments to offer online — services, everything from obtaining permits and licenses to paying taxes. The company rolled through $40 million worth of venture capital in 18 months, unable to overcome the expense of unanticipated client needs, high operating costs, and a frozen equity market.

One of govWorks' cost-related problems that could have been solved earlier by asking the right questions (see below) was the decision to host applications in-house. This proved extremely expensive and time-consuming. With the company's first large restructuring and subsequent layoffs, they moved to the ASP (application service provider) model. They hoped to be able to cut costs substantially by using an ASP.

But it was too little, too late. Their competitors were offering the same services for less money or, in some cases, for free. By January 2001 the company had filed for Chapter 11 bankruptcy.

By following the checklist and questions listed below, a project manager can avoid at least some of the potential cost-driven pitfalls inherent in any project.

USING A COST ESTIMATES CHECKLIST

Invalid cost estimates are considered one of the three major causes of project failure. However, the source of the failure may be because of two factors: invalid time estimates (Chapter 5A) and the assumption that costs are discrete data; that is, you do not need a range of costs. The example Checklist for Cost Estimates given in Chapter 28A is used to consider both of these problems.

Even when there is a single piece of hardware with a "fixed" catalogue value, there has to be a cost estimate that includes the three scenarios; that is pessimistic, realistic, and optimistic. The pessimistic estimate would include the effects of not having the hardware, while the optimistic considers having an even better piece of hardware if it is available. The estimate also has to consider the factor of how fixed is "fixed." The example checklist with its instructions considers these situations when doing cost estimating.

If you consider especially the pessimistic scenario for a cost estimate, then you have a basis for a contingency plan. Within a company, there is usually a broad policy on the creating of an annual group budget by headcount (employees) rather than by skill levels. It is recognized that the corporate budgetary policy might distinguish between a junior programmer and a senior programmer, but ignores the reality that there might be major skill differences within each group. Because the factor of skill levels is important to the project management process, the checklist instructions show you how you consider this issue. A contingency plan might be a pessimistic cost estimate scenario of the loss of an essential skill. You would have to factor in the cost by using a temporary worker from an outside source.

The first assumption for the design and development of the checklist and its instructions is that there must be a separate Project Budget, even if in actuality the various budget items are "hidden" within the IS group's budget because of corporate constraints. You must have a separate management document so you can properly manage the financial issues.

WARNING: Shoddy cost estimates impact the Project Budget in the same manner as inferior time estimates impact the Project Schedule. However, there is one big difference: Uupper level management tends to view a schedule as a management tool, but a budget is a document that is set in stone unless management wants to change the document. This actuality must be considered a major constraint for any project cost estimating.

USING ESSENTIAL DEFINITIONS

All prior discussions on estimates are relevant to this chapter, especially those in Chapter 5A on time estimates. The following seven definitions; however, are essential to any discussion about cost estimates:

Cost estimating is the process of establishing or defining the amount to be budgeted for a task based on constraints and assumptions from the project goals for the duration of the task, the average skills required for completing the task, and the resources required for completing the task.

An **estimate** is a guess based on opinion or a forecast based on experience. Cost, time, and resource estimates are the foundations for project planning.

Padding is an informal action such as adding time or cost to an estimate, that should not take place. Any such estimates should be formalized in a contingency plan.

A **resource** is anything that supports the project. This includes, in general terms, money, skills, materials, time, facilities, and equipment.

The Project Cost Updates document updates the initial project cost estimates at each major phase of implementation with comparison to the Initial Budget Estimate.

ADDING SUPPORTIVE DEFINITIONS

Many of the 36 concepts noted here are the same as those listed in Chapter 5A on time estimates. All project estimates work similarly to the fingers of your hands; that is in an independent but integrated manner.

An **activity** at the operational level (a task at the tactical level) is the effort required to achieve a measurable result that uses time and resources.

A **baseline plan** is the initial approved point from which any deviations will be determined using standards and benchmarks.

A **benchmark** is a specific technical level of excellence.

The **Budget** is a plan where costs are organized into debits and credits (expenses and revenues). It is a formal plan that uses a chart of accounts to give structure to estimates.

Budgeting is entering cost estimates into a formal financial structure.

The **Business Justification** is the general rationale for making the financial investment.

The **Business Justification Update** document ensures that the current view of the implementation of any project goals have performance criteria to meet previous commitments and management expectations.

The **Commercial Specification** is an evolution of the Business Justification. It identifies the market needs and gives adequate requirement and limitation data for the design and development group(s).

A **cost-benefit analysis** is the development of a ratio to determine if a project is financially viable.

A **critical activity** or task if not completed means project failure.

A **deliverable** is a clearly defined project result, product, or service.

Dependency means that a task has to be completed before a succeeding task can be completed. For example, coding has to be completed before code testing can be completed.

The **Design and Development Plan** drives the project Integration Plan that captures all major design and development deliverables and milestones for management tracking and reporting.

Duration is the total involved time of an activity or a task, including production-time and wait-time.

Extrapolation modeling is the theoretical process of extending historical data.

The **Field Introduction Requirements** document reflects the strategy and detailed plans to verify conformance to specification and functionality as defined in the Project Specification.

Headcount is a factor used by business managers in planning an annual budget but should not be used by project managers.

The **Initial Budget Estimates** provides a view of the expected development costs. Estimates are usually based on the Preliminary Project Specification. This document is updated in the Project Cost Update.

The **Initial Funding Requirements** document is for monitoring and reporting project costs at each major phase of implementation. It should include comparisons to the original funding document used to establish financial targets and expected milestones and deliverables. This document can also be included in the Project Cost Update.

A **learning curve** is a graphical representation of repetitive tasks that, when done on a continuous basis, lead to a reduction in activity duration, resources, and costs.

Leveling is the technique used to smooth out peaks and valleys for the use of resources.

Logistics is the process of getting the correct resource to the correct location at the correct time.

A **management review** is a regularly scheduled performance review.

The **Market Analysis Report** documents and verifies market opportunities and justifies the features, services, and applications for the project goals.

An **optimistic estimate** is an assumption that holds that everything will go as planned.

Performance is the measurable level of action to achieve a measurable project goal. It is the act or level of work demonstrated and judged based on identified skill level.

A **pessimistic estimate** is an assumption that if something can go wrong, it will.

The **Project Support Plan** ensures that the project is supportable in a market environment. This plan should include a process for customer support.

A **quality audit** is an independent evaluation or test of some component of the project by qualified personnel.

A **realistic estimate** is an assumption that there will probably be a few difficulties, but with compromise, the difficulties will be overcome.

Scheduling is the task that formalizes the time estimates within a calendar structure. It is an integration of sequencing tasks, resource planning, cost estimating, and time estimating.

Skill level is a factor used by a project manager in planning the project's Budget rather than using headcount.

Time estimating is concerned with the duration of an individual activity or groups of related activities (tasks).

A **trade-off** is an act of balancing project constraints.

The **Trial (Beta) Strategy** identifies the software and hardware elements in the project that are a part of any trial.

Variance is any deviation from the planned work whether it is cost, time, or resources.

COMPARING COST ESTIMATES TO THE BUDGET

There are two keystones to a successful project: reliable time (Chapter 5A) and cost estimates. The keyword is "reliable," the old process adage of "garbage in, garbage out" is especially true here. The important baseline of successful cost estimating is not to include padding, but to create a contingency plan. A cost estimate is indirectly padded when its related time estimate has been padded. The processes of cost estimating and budgeting are not the same function, and there is more to the process than simply formalizing cost estimates into the Budget. When you think about cost estimates, they are on an activity level first and then are grouped at the project task level. The Budget should only use tasks. Here are 10 comparisons between cost estimating and budgeting:

1. Cost estimates are inputs into a budget, while budget items are inputs into a table of accounts.

2. The project manager and operational managers look at cost estimates, while any number of upper level managers looks at the Budget.

3. Cost estimates reflect the financial aspect of tasks, while a budget is a plan to be followed.

4. Cost estimating is a component of budgeting; budgeting is the formal structuring of groups of tasks that includes those of a project at one level of the corporate budget.

5. Cost estimating is a consequence of analyzing; budgeting is a consequence of planning.

6. Cost estimating is at times nebulous, while budgeting is at times definite.

7. Cost estimating is first concerned with an individual activity and then the tasks of related activities, while budgeting is concerned with the complete project.

8. Cost estimating is to the Budget as time estimating is to the Schedule.

9. Cost estimating is viewed as an abstract process, while budgeting is viewed as a concrete process.

10. Cost estimating uses the duration (production- and wait-times) of a single activity or a task, while budgeting is the formal process used to frame the spending plan within a calendar usually based on monthly increments and accounting categories.

The above 10 comparisons could be stated as a comparison of the project manager's financial view and the business manager's financial view. The Budget is frequently taken to be written in concrete until the fourth quarter. Unfortunately, projects cannot be based on a monthly, quarterly, or annual increments. The successful completion of a project has to be considered in the context of its reliable time and cost estimates rather than on schedule and budget.

> The usual project management statement is that the project must be completed on time and under budget. This is a mixing of apples and oranges. Apples are the estimates for costs and time; oranges are a schedule and a budget.

REFINING DATA BY ASKING THE CORRECT QUESTIONS

Questions for cost estimating should be based on identified benchmarks, that is a measurable activity or task, whenever possible. These questions need to reflect managing of actual, specific expenses (costs) against planned costs (budget). By asking questions about the cost estimating process, you can formulate the data types required for your management forms and checklists for this area.

The responses to the following questions should be based on the goals and deliverables for your project, and the activities or tasks necessary to achieve them. Think in terms both of an optimistic cost and a pessimistic cost, and then determine a reliable median cost. Cost estimate should be a range rather than a single value. You will still need an absolute total at the end of the range, but at least you will have a value that is pessimistic. This principle can be used to reduce padding and to create a financial contingency plan.

> Unfortunately, one cost-estimating practice is to give a value without stating the impact of production- and wait-times.

In Chapter 5A, the approach used for developing questions on time estimates reflected the importance of impacts. The following 20 questions reflect the general cost estimating process to define data types:

1. How do cost estimates reflect final project goals?
2. How does the use of a chart of accounts affect the cost estimating process?

3. How have possible increases or decreases in prices been factored into the process of developing the original cost estimates?

4. How should cost estimates be reviewed?

5. What are the communications costs for tasks such as notification of project status?

6. What are the criteria for determining whether a known cost outweighs a known or potential threat, which can turn into a risk?

7. What are the objective criteria for establishing reliable cost estimates?

8. What critical estimates are based on the results of a Critical Path Method action?

9. What are the impacts of the quality control benchmarks and validation processes on project costs?

10. What are the ranges of rates of the outside services for a skill or equipment?

11. What are the types of inputs that must be considered for an activity or a task?

12. When should an outside expert be used to do cost estimating?

13. When should cost estimates be reviewed?

14. When should only internal resources be used?

15. Where in the process should base cost estimates be determined on average production?

16. Who is going to fund the various project tasks?

17. Who is to do the cost estimating for an activity or a task?

18. Who should review the cost estimates?

19. Why should all individual cost estimates be determined before doing a total estimate?

20. Why should the revised cost estimates be from the lowest to the highest?

As stated in the prior chapters, each of these questions could be reformulated in the context of any of the six metaquestions — how?, why?, when?, where?, who?, and what?.

USING THE FORM AND CHECKLIST PROCESS

Data types for cost estimates evolve out of the Scope Plan (project goals, assumptions, and constraints), the Activity Plan, and most directly from the time and resource estimates. Using these sources plus the questions presented above on the cost estimating process. You can develop a list of the many data types you will need to do cost estimating. The following list gives only 10 of these many data types:

1. Cost estimates based on skill types and levels rather than on head-count

2. Cost estimates that reflect the methodical nature of procurement

3. Criteria for associating cost and time estimates and potential changes

4. Criteria for establishing cost measures

5. Criteria for formulating cost estimates

6. Methodology for validating cost estimates according to the goals of your project

7. Policy on notifying others of cost changes to the project process

8. Procedure for associating cost estimates with people, and equipment and people acquisition

9. Quality management and validation cost estimates (which should be 10 to 20% of the total cost estimates)

10. Specific cost estimates for handling risks (threats and opportunities)

In Chapter 28A it has an example checklist with instructions for assisting you in developing reliable cost estimates. Beyond the standard optimistic, realistic, and pessimistic cost estimates, it is critical to have measurable and objective criteria for determining any cost estimate. The Critical Path Method establishes the beginning point in the cost estimates for activities or tasks and times.

07costf — Cost Estimates Checklist

07costi — Instructions for a Cost Estimates Checklist

Chapter 8A

Defining and Managing a Project Budget

OBJECTIVES: At the end of this chapter, you will be able to:

- State how using a Project Budget rather an IS budget can benefit a project manager.
- Identify 30 concepts that are appropriate for developing a set of questions used for establishing the Budget.
- Develop the skill to use an interrogative process to create budget items.
- Learn to differentiate between a budget and a set of cost estimates.
- Become aware of how to develop a checklist that can be used to design and develop a Project Budget.

Like the Schedule, the Project Budget is a visual representation; it illustrates the various cost estimates that make up the financial underpinnings of the project. But when projects start to run over time and over cost, the project manager must make crucial decisions that may not have been factored into the original budget planning.

The Budget, like the Schedule, is an overall set of estimates that is not set in stone but must be defined and refined, sometimes while managing the project. Such a possibility must be part of any contingency planning.

Practically speaking, a budget helps you keep tabs on one fundamental question: *Are cost estimates correct?*

For example, a mid-sized software development company specializing in financial services applications began work on a new product for its banking clients. After six months of development, the project was running over the original time and budget estimates. The project and product managers insisted on training more developers in order to roll out the product, but the cost of the high learning curve set the project back even further and the Budget had to be completely revised. Eventually, a new project manager whose view was more in line with that of company management was brought onboard.

This is a parallel discussion to Chapter 6A on the development of the Project Schedule.

USING A PROJECT BUDGET RATHER THAN AN IS BUDGET

The essential assumption of this chapter and its associated checklist (Chapter 28A) for the design and development of budgetary items is that there must a separate Project Budget. It does not necessarily have to be a part of the formal budget structure of the company, but it would make project management — and perhaps even the managing of your IS financial issues — much easier.

The checklist assists you in your design and development of a budget. You might also use the company's format to assist you. A Project Budget gives the visual financial status of your project and supportive evidence in a set of documents. It includes the source of funds, the amount to be spent by major task groups, and the month in which it is to be spent. If the financial components of a project are "hidden" within single or multiple lines of an IS budget, you have to struggle to keep matters correct. When you are asked to revisit your IS budget on a quarterly basis by your upper level management, how do you distinguish easily between the amounts that belong to the project and to the IS group? If an edict comes down from upper-level management that you must cut all budget lines by 10%, what do you do? If you do this automatically, how does it impact the project? The checklist gives you a tool to lessen the impact of such an edict, and it assists you in protecting the budgetary items for the project.

Using this methodology, I kept up with 18 different sized projects at one time. At the end of the year, I knew within $50 what was actually spent on each project by funding source, and by the group as funded by the corporation.

USING ESSENTIAL DEFINITIONS

Because a budget is, first, a visual presentation of the cost-oriented efforts of a project and, second, is a project standard or baseline for managing a project, it involves a large number of essential concepts related to budgeting. Here are of the eight essential concepts. (The list actually could be longer because any project document probably has financial data that is relevant to the project budget.):

A **baseline plan** is the initial approved point from which any deviations will be determined using standards and benchmarks.

The **Budget** is a plan where costs are organized into debits and credits (expenses and revenues). It is a formal plan that uses a chart of accounts to give structure to estimates for expenses and revenues.

Budgeting is entering cost estimates into a formal financial structure.

An **estimate** is a guess based on opinion or a forecast based on experience. Cost, time, and resource estimates are the foundations for project planning.

Headcount is a factor used by business managers in planning an annual budget but should not be used by project managers.

The **Initial Budget Estimates** provides a view of the expected development costs. Estimates are usually based on the Preliminary Project Specification. This document is updated in the Project Cost Update.

Padding is an informal action, such as adding time or cost to an estimate, that should not take place. Any such estimates should be formalized as in a contingency plan.

Skill level is a factor used by a project manager in planning the project's Budget, rather than using headcount.

ADDING SUPPORTIVE DEFINITIONS

Besides the 8 concepts listed above, here are additional 22 definitions:

An **assumption** is a prediction that something will be true, either an action or an event that ensures project success.

Authority is the investment in managing and controlling a series of tasks such as a project.

The **Business Justification** is the general rationale for making the financial investment.

The **Business Justification Update** document ensures the current view of the implementation of any project goals have performance criteria to meet previous commitments and management expectations.

The **Commercial Specification** is an evolution of the Business Justification. It identifies the market need and gives adequate requirement and limitation data for the design and development group(s).

Contingency is the rational preparation for change.

A **contingency plan** is the preparation for a pessimistic scenario to become reality.

A **cost-benefit analysis** is the development of a ratio to determine if a project is financially viable.

Cost estimating is the process of establishing or defining the amount to be budgeted for a task based on constraints and assumptions from the project goals for the duration of the task, the average skills required in completing the task, and the resources required in completing the task.

The **Design and Development Plan** drives the project Integration Plan that captures all major design and development deliverables and milestones for management tracking and reporting.

Extrapolation modeling is the theoretical process of extending historical data.

A **gate** is another term for milestone or a major project event.

The **Initial Funding Requirements** document is for monitoring and reporting project costs at each major phase of implementation. It should include comparisons to the original funding document used to establish financial targets and expected milestones and deliverables. This document can also be included in the Project Cost Update.

Logistics is the process of getting the correct resource to the correct location at the correct time.

An **optimistic estimate** is an assumption that holds that everything will go as planned.

An **organization chart** is normally a visual representation of who reports to whom. It shows the hierarchical and perhaps functional relationships among organizational groups. The project organization chart must include the core project responsibilities of each team member.

A **pessimistic estimate** is an assumption that if something can go wrong, it will.

The **Project Cost Updates** document updates the initial project cost estimates at each major phase of implementation with comparison to the Initial Budget Estimate.

A **realistic estimate** is an assumption that there will probably be a few difficulties, but with compromise, the difficulties will be overcome.

The **Schedule** is the duration of the project, including production-time and wait-time. It is also a production plan for the allocation of tasks with deadlines.

Slippage (budget) is when a budget item is overspent.

Slippage (time) is expected when you know about it before the due date; it is unexpected when you learn about it after-the-fact, that is after the due date.

COMPARING THE BUDGET TO COST ESTIMATES

You need either an informal or formal Project Budget. It is most likely you will have to create your own informal budget; that is, a document that is based on your corporate chart of accounts and that combines all the various formal budgets related to the project. An unfortunate practice is to enter individual project budget items as one combined item in your IS group budget or in the formal budget of each participating group of the project team.

To comprehend a budget in the context of its inputs of cost estimates, you must be aware of some of the differences between a project budget and a business budget. The following 10 comparisons show some of the differences:

1. A project budget cannot easily be used to determine unpredictable peak periods, while a business budget can be created to manage peak periods such as Christmas sales or end-of-quarter requirements.

2. A project budget cannot survive on unrealistic estimates, while a business budget might (the reason for third- and fourth-quarter reviews of budgets).

3. A project budget does not need to consider long-term benefits, while a business budget usually does.

4. A project budget is concerned with achieving goals, while a business budget focuses on profit.

5. A project budget relies on contract services more than a business budget.

6. A project budget requires a place for contingencies, while a business budget usually does not.

7. A project budget requires money to maximize resources, while the business budget includes baselines for minimum resources.

8. A project budget should be based on skill requirements, while a business budget uses headcount.

9. A project budget usually has limited financial histories to use as an estimating tool, while a business budget usually has, at minimum, last year's budget to use for planning or for financial histories with similar functions.

10. A project budget usually reflects costs for highly skilled personnel, while a business budget hides skill differences.

As a project manager, you must recognize that you are working with estimates, not with an absolute set of costs. Unfortunately, there exists an attitude that the Schedule and especially the Budget are set in concrete. You need to have as many project budget items as possible so you are able to manage the quarterly changes. When you only have one budget item, how do you manage a cut of 20% and make changes quickly?

Several years ago, partners at a large international accounting firm decided to implement a popular new technology to deliver an on-line magazine to subscribers. Weeks before the launch, the company that produced the technology teetered on the edge of bankruptcy, foiled by an unstable and technologically restrictive product despite advertising spin and good word-of-mouth. The on-line project had to be redesigned for delivery using a different technology. It blew the budget and precipitated one of the worst scenarios possible for a project manager.

REFINING DATA BY ASKING THE CORRECT QUESTIONS

The core question for the design, development, and implementation of any budget is "What method should I use to ensure that the project's budget is minimally impacted by the business budget cycle?" You need realistic cost data to defend your budget.

The following 20 questions as in prior chapters reflect the use of the 6 basic metaquestions. Because the Budget along with your Schedule are your prime project management tools for administering the process, you must consider the purpose, actor, location, time range, method, and justification for any project activity or task. You should ask questions that clarify an issue, not muddle it.

1. How and to whom is financial information given?
2. How will budget items be consistent to the project's goals and objectives and reflect the customer's needs?
3. How are internal and external resources budgeted?
4. How are project cost estimates to be allocated?
5. How are various budgets interrelated?
6. How has the quality management process been cost estimated and budgeted?
7. How many budgets are affected by this project?
8. What are the impacts on the budgetary process for outsourcing tasks?
9. What are the budget lines for support functions such as documentation and training?
10. What is the defined duration of the project?
11. What is the procedure for handling payments for outside resources?
12. When should there be links between the project's budget and any other budgets?
13. When should there be separate budget lines for quality control and assurance?

14. Where do project budget items "go" in a formal budgetary structure?
15. Where is the project's budget is an item for risk management?
16. Where have potential risks been factored into the budgetary process?
17. Who approves the project's budget?
18. Who communicates changes and updates to the budget reporting system as relevant to the project's change management?
19. Who is responsible for managing the project's budget cycle when it impacts another budget over several of its cycles?
20. Who is responsible for resolving the project's budget when formal corporate quarterly changes happen?

USING THE FORM AND CHECKLIST PROCESS

You have made the first step in gathering data when you have recognized that a budget is more than just a formal plan divided into monthly expenses and revenues and budget item lines. It requires supporting details to properly manage the financial aspect of a project. A budget has the highest level of "rollup."

You may find that salvation, not the devil, is found in the details. You need a form or a checklist that assists you in ensuring that you have adequate financial details. Sources for data that can be used in the budget process might come from these documents:

- Business Justification and Its Update
- Commercial Specification
- Design and Development Plan
- Initial Budget Estimates
- Initial Funding Requirements
- Project Cost Update

In Chapter 28A the following form and its instructions can be used to develop a comprehensive budget definition process:

08budf — Checklist for Project Budget Items

08budi — Instructions for a Project Budget Checklist

Chapter 9A

Managing Quality Control and Assurance

OBJECTIVES: At the end of this chapter, you will be able to:

- State a rationale for using a checklist to develop a quality management program.
- Define the importance of measuring intangible effects on the IS infrastructure and project results.
- Identify 50 concepts that can be used for a discussion on a quality management process or program.
- Develop the skill to use an interrogative process to establish a reliable quality management process.
- Develop a framework for creating a checklist that can refine a quality management program or process.

The Y2K phenomenon, as it became known, left a legacy in the IS world that continues to resonate deeply. It demonstrated the need for disaster recovery plans and for tight quality assurance, especially in the present environment where there is a constant challenge to work on faster schedules and in exponentially more complex environments.

As an example illustration the importance of QA: Public Service Electric and Gas, New Jersey's largest power utility, set up a permanent quality assurance department to test all new software. The objective was to replicate the successful team of QA engineers who performed tests on the Year 2000 work of programmers. Previously, programmers had done all testing of the utility's software.

Quality management issues can be viewed as either a cost center or profit maker for any business. It is costly because you must hire highly skilled professionals to do the work who must be involved from the initial project phase onward. As well any failure to meet customer requirements can be costly on the business side. But QA that maintains a quality standard for your products or services is profitable because it helps brand your company as professional. And active quality management program can bring you huge savings by identifying serious errors in your products or services before they are released to the market.

USING A QUALITY MANAGEMENT PROGRAM CHECKLIST

As has been stated quite a number of times invalid time and cost estimates are two of the primary reasons for the failure of most projects. The actual reason for project failure may because of the lack of an early warning system. An early warning system is, in reality, an effective quality management program that has two major functions: control and assurance. Most managers say they have a quality control program: actually, they probably have a loosely defined framework that is not integrated into the project management process. Too many project managers reply purely on the corporate and IS quality groups to handle project issues without direction. The rationale is that these groups know their jobs, so why should the project manager need to tell them anything?

The big failure is when a quality group is not brought into the very beginnings of a project, and is usually called upon only when there is a problem or pain caused by a potential risk. You do preventive maintenance on your car: should you not do the same for a project? When a quality group sits too far from the project manager, their input is overlooked until, the traditional events for validation and testing are to occur. Unfortunately, these are the times when project managers usually find the dark goblins in the closet.

Two of the essential items in the creation of time and cost estimates are reliable and relevant standards and benchmarks. The checklist and its instructions should assist you in integrating the quality functions into these efforts. Without this integration, you should expect risks and possible project failure.

The Quality Management checklist should be used to identify the most intangible effects on the IS infrastructure and the project's results. These intangibles include innovation, interoperability, reliability, scalability, stakeholder satisfaction, and production quality. When these intangibles are ignored, there is the potential for long-   range effects beyond the project's duration with the IS group. In addition, all forms of information gathering should be considered: formal technical meetings, review briefings, reports (paper, e-mail, and bulletin boards), and — perhaps the most powerful form of information gathering — hallway conversations.

A special task that specifically relates to the IS group is for Quality Management to determine technical performances for configuration management. All hardware and software have to be integrated correctly. One of the most dangerous activities is when a programmer does "cut and paste," which means taking a piece of code created for one specific function and replicating it for some other function to meet a project's goal. The technical performance requirement is to determine the effects of this replicated code — it might cause a database value to be processed incorrectly or may change the code processing sequence.

USING ESSENTIAL DEFINITIONS

The 5 essential concepts that are the basis for any discussion on a quality control and assurance program are the following:

Quality assurance is based on performance. It is the establishing of performance standards, then measuring and evaluating project performance against these standards. This component of quality management considers measurable deviations in performance during a project.

A **quality audit** is an independent evaluation or test of some component of the project by qualified personnel.

Quality control is the component of quality management that considers the system or development processes of a project. It is the tasks used to meet standards through the gathering of performance information, inspecting, monitoring, and testing.

Quality management is the process that uses control and assurance to prevent risks and, if a risk occurs, to minimize it.

The **Quality Plan** defines the role of Quality Control and Assurance in all phases of the project process.

ADDING SUPPORTIVE DEFINITIONS

In addition to the 5 concepts given above, here are 45 more supporting concepts for the discussion on quality control and assurance:

Accountability is the act of accepting the responsibility for the results of an act whether it is a success or failure.

An **activity** at the operational level (a task at the tactical level) is the effort required to achieve a measurable result that uses time and resources.

Advising is giving general rather than specific directions, evaluating, giving an option, or instructing.

An **assumption** is a prediction that something will be true, either an action or an event that ensures project success, such as, "There will be identified potential risks, but somehow they will be overcome."

An **audit** is a formal study of the project as a whole, or a project's component, as to status (progress and results), costs, and procedures.

A **baseline plan** is the initial approved point from which any deviations will be determined using standards and benchmarks.

A **benchmark** is a specific technical level of excellence.

Compromising is a skill set that seeks a win-win situation.

Conflict is an action of opposing ideas or positions. It is an imbalance among available skills, priorities, or resources.

A **constraint** is a parameter, limitation, or boundary for the project plan such as the Budget or the Schedule.

A **contingency plan** is the preparation for a pessimistic scenario to become reality.

Control is the monitoring of progress and the checking for variances in the plan.

A **critical activity** or task if not completed means project failure.

A **deliverable** is a clearly defined project result, product, or service.

Dependency means that a task has to be completed before a succeeding task can be completed. For example, coding has to be completed before code testing can be completed.

An **estimate** is a guess based on opinion, or a forecast based on experience. Cost, time, and resource estimates are the foundations for project planning.

Expectation is a stated project goal that can become a perceived undocumented result.

Feedback is an activity that should be held on a regular basis in which the status of the person being evaluated can be clearly stated based on measurable standards or benchmarks.

The **International Organization for Standardization** (ISO) is a consortium that sets standards in a variety of areas.

ISO 9000 is a quality system standard for any product, service, or process.

ISO 9001 is a quality system standard for design, production, and installation of a product or service.

ISO 9002 is a quality system model for quality assurance in production and installation.

ISO 9003 is a quality system model for quality assurance in final inspection and testing.

ISO 9004 is a set of quality management guidelines for any organization to use to develop and implement a quality system.

Leveling is the technique used to smooth out peaks and valleys for the use of resources.

Line-staff conflicts are differences of opinion and ideas between horizontal management levels.

Logistics is the process of getting the correct resource to the correct location at the correct time.

A **management review** is a regularly scheduled performance review.

A **milestone** is a clearly defined date of start or date of 100% completion.

A **model** is a theoretical environment with as much data as possible to reflect reality adequately for decision-making.

An **opportunity** is a situation that will positively affect the project in time, money, resources, or all three in a significant manner.

An **optimistic estimate** is an assumption that holds that everything will go as planned.

Padding is an informal action, such as adding time or cost to an estimate, that should not take place. Any such estimates should be formalized in a contingency plan.

Performance is the measurable level of action to achieve a measurable project goal. It is the act or level of work demonstrated and judged based on identified skill level.

A **pessimistic estimate** is an assumption that if something can go wrong, it will.

PMI stands for the Project Management Institute, a professional organization that studies and promotes project management.

Process is a systematic and sequential set of activities (tasks) to achieve a set of measurable goals.

Program Evaluation and Review Technique (PERT) was developed for the United States Department of Defense in the late 1950s. Specifically it was developed by the consulting firm of Booz, Allen, and Hamilton for the U.S. Navy's Polaris submarine project (Polaris Weapon System). It combines statistics and network diagrams.

A **realistic estimate** is an assumption that there will probably be a few difficulties, but with compromise, the difficulties will be overcome.

A **risk** is a performance error that can have a significant or disastrous impact on the success of a project or major task. It is more than a problem; its effect can have an adverse or disastrous consequence on the project's outcome.

A **scenario** is a set of possibilities that could happen to cause a risk.

Simulation is a process to imitate the physical components of your informational system.

A **standard** is usually external, industry-accepted document for achieving quality for the one or more of the project-defined expected goals.

The **Trial (Beta) Strategy** identifies the software and hardware elements in the project that are a part of any trial. The "where," the "when," and the "whom" should be included in the strategy. This provides a clear identification of the testing requirements plus the extent of the resources and capabilities necessary to trial.

Variance is any deviation from the planned work whether it is cost, time, or resources.

A few factors are necessary to improving quality control and assurance: frequent communications among testing, development, business and operations groups; shorter cycles and smaller releases; skilled IT professionals; and training in new technologies.

REFINING DATA BY ASKING THE CORRECT QUESTIONS

Any quality program has two components — control and assurance. Often, one talks of a quality program, one says "quality control." But, because, a quality program is two-headed function, the phrase should really be "quality management." You must consider both functions — defining and doing or monitoring and measuring.

"Control" carries with it a negative connotation these days. The concept was originally developed because a group of people on a manufacturing floor watched over (controlled) the production process. This concept has been altered with the passing of time, since today's production process is more nebulous. The emphasis is now on results such as how well a software utility handles defined functions. More often than not the process for programming the utility is ignored.

After you can have control — the gathering of standards and other data to define quality — you must have assurance. Quality assurance's baseline is based on measurable performance; it involves finding and establishing performance standards, then establishing the project quality baseline against these standards. This component of quality management considers measurable deviations in performance during a project. The real function of quality assurance is what most people think of as quality control.

You can ask any number of questions on quality assurance and, from those responses, you determine your data types and data requirements. After you have determined your required benchmarks and standards, you then use them to determine local performance requirements. This task is very important, because these requirements must match the project's goals. Even when you use a standard for more than one project, you may have to add or eliminate data types. The following 10 questions consider the structure of a quality assurance effort or process.

1. How do the project's milestones impact the quality assurance process?

2. How should quality assurance personnel be selected?

3. What are the qualitifcations for a person to be a member of the quality assurance team?

4. What are the performance criteria for selecting the logical set of benchmarks and standards for the project?

5. What are the documentation and training requirements for the quality assurance program?

6. What quality assurance functions have to be cost estimated and budgeted?

7. When should the quality assurance program be established?

8. Where should the quality assurance function be located?

9. Who should be responsible for the quality assurance process?

10. Why should the quality assurance program be established?

For both quality assurance and control, you will need to use the metaquestions discussed in the prior chapters. Because quality is ultimately customer satisfaction, you need to know purposes, actors, and methods.

Next is quality control, which is performed not only by a team of specialists, but by the project team as a whole. The project team must extend itself across group boundaries. The following questions should be answered in broad terms by the project team, while the special quality control team should answer the questions in specific terms:

1. How have the quality control procedures been cost estimated and budgeted?
2. How should the quality control program identify procedural standards and performance benchmarks, and then link them to project goals?
3. What are the criteria for documenting quality control tasks?
4. What are the impacts of quality control on time estimates?
5. What are the impacts on training requirements because of quality control?
6. What are the quality control procedures that ensure correct sequencing?
7. What is the necessary time for quality identification?
8. What quality control events have to be included at project milestones?
9. When should ISO standards be used?
10. When should the defined standards and benchmarks be used?

Based on the responses to these two sets of 10 questions, you can formulate the requirements for the project's quality processes and in addition, the required data types and data. These data types and data requirements become the backdrop for shaping the project's quality management function. For example, when you identify a specific benchmark, you will also know some of data you must collect by project task to determine if that task has met the performance benchmark.

USING THE FORM AND CHECKLIST PROCESS

Your interrogative process is used to establish an environment for you to identify necessary data types and data not establish them *per se*. Thus, your first activity is to design and develop a checklist to ensure that you have found all the appropriate sources for determining quality management data types and data requirements. In Chapter 28A is a more comprehensive checklist for handling this task.

The checklist reflects a series of activities such as identifying a standard. The use of the whole checklist can be considered a task that is quality management or two tasks — one for control, the other for assurance.

Some of the important sources used to manage this task include the following:

- Project goals
- Performance benchmark requirements
- Procedural standards requirements
- ISO standards
- Corporate administrative and technical policies
- Validation requirements
- Vendor documentation
- Documentation requirements
- Training requirements
- Resource requirements (compatibility, interoperability, and portability)

Do not forget the two most important project baselines for data — time and cost estimates. This process is governed by an essential goal — to ensure data consistency — which is really product consistency or, even better, customer satisfaction.

Ultimately, Quality Management seeks to monitor, evaluate, validate, and test:

- Tasks that are being completed in accordance with or better than standards and benchmarks.
- Tasks that are not being completed in accordance with standards and benchmarks.
- Potential opportunities that might change the Project Schedule or Project Budget.
- Tasks that affect the intangibles of the IS infrastructure.

- Performance that has to be recorded for use in the company on a regular basis.

- Tasks that are meeting or not meeting the company's strategic and operational goals.

- Project effectiveness and efficiency that can impact project results.

- Events that impact the IS group's relationships with other functional groups.

- Events that impact customer satisfaction.

In Chapter 28A the following form and its instructions will assist you in detailing the required data types and data:

09QCf — Checklist for a Quality Management Program

09QCi — Instructions for the Quality Management Checklist

Chapter 10A

Managing Risk

OBJECTIVES: At the end of this chapter, you will be able to:

- State the primary benefits and consequences of the use of a checklist for a risk management process.
- Identify 24 concepts for the development of a set of questions used to create basic criteria for establishing a risk management process.
- Develop the skill to use an interrogative process to refine the criteria for a risk management process that is trustworthy.
- Learn that risk and opportunity are the two faces of the same coin.
- Become aware of how to develop a checklist to develop better risk management tasks.

Recently an e-mail spun around in Internet circles admonishing Hotmail users that their e-mail could be read by any semi-skilled hacker. Indeed, there are a couple of sites that give specific instructions on how to do so. For those who rely on Web e-mail because it provides easy access from almost any Web browser, the realization that opportunity and risk are two faces of the same coin comes as a blow.

In a world of increasing technological complexity, the project manager who tries to manage risk effectively may turn to new technologies for help, but introducing such new factors may bring different forms of risk. So it is with the ASP (Application Service Provider) model, which increases the distribution of applications and limits the amount of physical software and hardware, thereby lowering costs to customers and possibly increasing confidence if the company is small or the costs too high. But ASPs also bring concerns about security and reliability.

The ASP purveyor owns the actual software and licenses the product, but the data resides on the ASP's server. The customer rents, or uses for free in the case of Hotmail, the use of the ASP and accesses it from a remote location. Hotmail functions as an ASP because you can access it from a Web browser; however your e-mail sits on their server, not on your local machine. If the ASP does not protect your e-mail adequately, the e-mail could be vulnerable to security concerns. A good ASP has a secure data center and redundancy connections to ensure reliability.

In addition, there are different kinds of ASP models — from Web-based applications that are built and run by the same company, to ASP-enabled solutions that are built by one company and hosted elsewhere. The type of model to use depends entirely on the size and needs of the business. The project manager would do well to use the following questions and checklists to evaluate risk when choosing an ASP or as a matter of fact, in any project situation in which risk is paramount.

CREATING A RISK MANAGEMENT CHECKLIST

Risk management is a 24X7 condition involving all project stakeholders. The checklist with its instructions is not focused on the need to set up an organization, but to establish an early warning system. There is one situation where the statement "One only grows when one takes a risk" is invalid, and that is for a project. All the checklists discussed previously really are ultimately concerned with risk management. This checklist is similar to a summary of previous checklists, but it has its own value as well. This checklist seeks to define a framework for eliminating disastrous outcomes. This means a project failure. This checklist will assist you in identifying a series of failing events that have deviated critically from project's goals, standards, and benchmarks. Risk management is a highly focused form of quality management, but only in the largest and most complex projects is an organizational function. The guiding principle of this checklist is to create an insurance policy against shoddy time, resource, and cost estimates.

USING ESSENTIAL DEFINITIONS

There are three essential concepts for this discussion:

A **risk** is a performance error that can have a significant or disastrous impact on the success of a project or major task. It is more than a problem; its effect can have an adverse or disastrous consequence on the project's outcome.

Risk management is the task where you identify a risk, assess a risk, and allocate resources to resolve the risk.

Risk analysis is a technique, tool, or method for assessing either quantitatively or qualitatively (or both) the impacts of an identified risk or a potential risk identified through a scenario.

ADDING SUPPORTIVE DEFINITIONS

In addition to the 3 essential concepts noted above, there are 21 others that are important to this discussion. Some of these concepts have appeared in earlier chapters; however, in this chapter they should be viewed in light of risks and opportunities.

Accountability is the act of accepting the responsibility for the results of an act whether it is a success or failure. The usual form is "I accept responsibility for the failure," or "The team accepts responsibility for the success."

An **assumption** is a prediction that something will be true, either an action or an event that ensures project success.

A **confidence level** is the acceptance level of risk usually determined statistically by a percentage of time or cost.

A **constraint** is a parameter, limitation, or boundary for the project plan such as the Budget or the Schedule.

Contingency is the rational preparation for change.

A **contingency plan** is the preparation for a pessimistic scenario to become reality.

A **critical activity** or task if not completed means project failure.

Criticality is a position on the team where the individual in this situation has specific skills; usually technical, that if not available to the project, puts the project at risk.

Dependency means that a task has to be completed before a succeeding task can be completed. For example, coding has to be completed before code testing can be completed.

Distortion is the misrepresentation of the situation whether it is a fact, experience, or feeling.

Effectiveness is the attained measure of quality to complete the activity, task, or event. It is also the skill required to define goals and to accomplish them.

Efficiency is the measurement of output based on amount of input. It is also the skill the can accomplish with a minimum of input to get a maximum of output.

Expectation is a stated project goal that can become a perceived undocumented result.

Line-staff conflicts are differences of opinion and ideas between horizontal management levels.

Logistics is the process of getting the correct resource to the correct location at the correct time.

A **management review** is a regularly scheduled performance review.

An **opportunity** is a situation that will positively affect the project in time, money, resources, or all three in a significant manner.

Performance is the measurable level of action to achieve a measurable project goal. It is the act or level of work demonstrated and judged based on identified skill level.

A **quality audit** is an independent evaluation or test of some component of the project by qualified personnel.

A **scenario** is a set of possibilities that could happen to cause a risk.

Variance is any deviation from the planned work whether it is cost, time, or resources.

SEEING RISKS AND OPPORTUNITIES AS TWINS

A risk is an adverse effect on a project; it is disastrous. There seem to be only checks for risks, but none for opportunities. An opportunity is not a simple change to the project process, but should be a significant affirming result to the project process that improves the company's bottom line. A risk or an opportunity can begin as a ripple and turn into a tidal wave. Both have to be managed. Thus, when you establish criteria for a risk, you must do the same for an opportunity. For every risk there may be a matching opportunity if you look deeper into the dark closet. The danger, of course, is the possibility that an opportunity is a disguised risk.

REFINING DATA BY ASKING THE CORRECT QUESTIONS

You should ask as many questions as you necessary to clarify a risk management environment; however, the following 6 questions must be asked up front:

1. What are the criteria for a risk?
2. Who defines the risk criteria?
3. When are the risk criteria applied?
4. Where in the project process are risk criteria applied?
5. How are the risk criteria applied?
6. Why has the potential risk happened?

Perhaps the first data type you need for risk management is a set of risk categories. Risks come in all colors and shapes. There are least eight common categories of risks, and you can easily add to them based on your specific project goals. Here is a short list of project risk categories:

1. Customer
   — Financial support becomes unavailable
   — Not participating in agreed upon reviews
   — Responses to questions are not timely

- New interpretations to goals
- Skill resources availability degrades

2. Delivery
   - Product does not meet functional requirements according to benchmarks, standards, or the project goals
   - Product has incompatibility issues
   - Product has interoperability issues
   - Product has portability issues
   - Product's capacity exceeds available capacity
   - Product's response time is inadequate

3. Equipment
   - Does not meet specifications
   - Limited availability
   - Missed delivery date

4. People
   - Lacking in skills required
   - Not available at time required
   - Not available because of job change

5. Physical
   - Critical computer or hardware failure
   - Data stolen
   - Facility lost through a catastrophe
   - Virus infects some critical data

6. Scope
   - Customer identifies the need for additional effort
   - New requirements are identified during development
   - An operational area introduces a new function that is not been approved by the project team

7. Technology
   - Technical assumptions are not factual
   - Technical constraints cannot be overcome

— Technology is not understood clearly

— Technology is too new

8. Vendor

— Financial failure

— Not participating in agreed-upon reviews

— Responses to questions are not timely

— New interpretations of support and goals

— Skill resources availability degrades

With the six core questions and these risk categories, you can make your first major step in identifying important risk data types and data requirements.

You can rewrite the above core questions and risk categories to reflect an opportunity. For example, the customer risk category could be stated as follows:

- Additional financial support becomes available
- Willing to participate in additional reviews
- Response time to questions exceeds expectations
- Accepts the interpretation of goals throughout the project
- Increases available skill resources

While you may consider the above situations pure fantasy, you must consider them at least on a theoretical basis. Considering any unexpected situation is the basis of risk management.

After you have examined the core questions, you have to ask questions about the risk management process you are going to use. If you have been thorough after this activity you are ready to determine your data types and data requirements. Here are 15 questions to ask on the risk management structure and process:

1. How does a contingency plan impact risk management?

2. How do cost estimates impact risk management?

3. How will the risk management tasks be funded?

4. What are the direct-cost estimates for risk management?

5. What are the documentation requirements for risk management?

6. What are the essential tasks for managing risks?

7. What are the resources required for risk management?

8. What skills and skill levels are required for risk management?

9. What are the time estimates for risk management?

10. What are the training requirements for risk management?

11. What procedures, benchmarks, standards, or policies govern risk management?

12. Where in the project budget is risk management allocated?

13. Where in the project process will there be assessments for risks?

14. Where in the project schedule are there appropriate links to the quality management schedule?

15. Who (which individual or group) is responsible for managing risks?

when "risk management" is used in the above questions, it is implied that risks and opportunities are discussed. When "risks" is used, it can be replaced by "opportunities."

USING THE FORM AND CHECKLIST PROCESS

One of the methods for acquiring data is to use a statistical model. This type of model uses mathematical distributions to define the performance of an activity or task. You, the IS manager, probably have more historical statistical data available that defines performance than any other manager. For example, you probably have available the following data to build a reliable network traffic model:

1. Bandwidth used

2. Circuit
   - Availability in %
   - Busy number (average, maximum)

- Failures (average maximum)
- Use in %

3. Number of calls (real, virtual)
   - Attempted
   - Blocked (failure, traffic)
   - Completed
   - Disconnected
   - Preempted
   - Queued

4. Number of packets
   - Blocked
   - Delivered
   - Processed
   - Transmitted

5. Call queue
   - Probability
   - Size
   - Time

6. Averages
   - Buffer use
   - Call length
   - Message delay
   - Packet delay
   - Packet queue time

It will always be easier to use technical data as benchmarks for identifying risks than to use data for "human" error. However, the essential action is to have measurable performance criteria. You need to have data that identify:

- Acceptable plus-or-minus measurable variances
- Assumptions

- Audit criteria
- Baselines for measuring effectiveness
- Baselines for measuring efficiencies
- Confidence levels
- Constraints
- Critical activities and tasks
- Distortion possibilities
- Logistic criteria
- Qualitative impacts
- Quantitative impacts

In Chapter 28A there are a form and its instructions that bring together to some extent the key ideas from the earlier forms and instructions to reflect the data types and data for risk management:

10Riskf — Checklist for Risk Management Tasks

10Riski — Instructions for a Risk Management Tasks Checklist

Section 5A

Project Management Forms, Checklists and Reflections

This section has example forms and instructions developed on the ideas in Section 1A. In addition, there is a chapter that is a set of reflections on the checklist process to identify types of data required to have a premium and qualitative project management process. These reflections are considered a framework for further thoughts on the project management process for IS professionals.

Chapter 28A, "Example Forms, Checklists, and Instructions," gives as the chapter title states. Its purpose is to ease the search for the forms and instructions throughout the book.

Chapter 29, "Reflections on the Checklist Process," summarizes major points in Section 1A to give a jumping off point for furthering your thinking is the realm of the IS project management process. It is a taste of the potential. In addition, there is a brief discussion of the influence of you skill sets on project form and checklist development.

"Skill sets" does means not a single skill such as a writing skill, but a group of skills that can be labeled such as organizer, negotiator, facilitator, or salesperson.

131

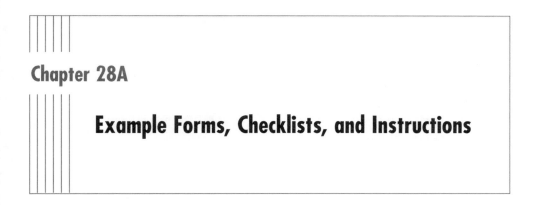

Chapter 28A

Example Forms, Checklists, and Instructions

OBJECTIVES: At the end of this chapter, you will be able to:

- Identify developed 10 forms and checklists as discussed in Section 1A.
- Compare 10 instructions to questionnaires and checklists for data assumptions and constraints.

These examples primarily focus on the planning, designing, developing, and implementing of a systematic IS project management process for qualitative measured goals. Using these checklists, you can easily develop local specific data collecting forms. There are many simple applications for creating these forms.

You might add an instruction when appropriate, such as "Give additional information on an attachment. State in the space, see attachment." Possible the most common special instruction in documenting is "Not applicable."

The responses to the later forms should be consistent with other earlier responses. For example, risk management tasks are listed throughout the other checklists, thus the Checklist for Risk Management Tasks is fundamentally a summary document for this particular function. The essential principle in accomplishing these checklists is not the amount of responses given, but consistency. The purpose of these checklists is to minimize or even prevent shoddy resource, time, and cost estimates.

01VIABLE CHECKLIST FOR PROJECT VIABILITY QUESTIONS

Measurable goals   _____
Acceptable assumptions   _____

Acceptable constraints   _____
Identified deliverables   _____
Identified risks   _____
Identified opportunities   _____
Identified project impacts   _____
Identified stakeholders   _____
Established project process   _____
Adequate duration   _____
Criteria for time estimates   _____
Schedule requirements   _____
Acceptable deadlines   _____
Cost-benefit analysis   _____
ROI impacts   _____
Adequate available funding
       Customer   _____
       IS   _____
       Other   _____
Budget requirements   _____
Criteria cost estimates   _____
Project authority adequate   _____
System infrastructure effects
       Compatibility   _____
Interoperability   _____
Portability   _____
Scalability   _____
Technology stability   _____
Quality control
       Identified process   _____
       External standards   _____
       Internal standards   _____
       External benchmarks   _____
       Internal benchmarks   _____
Quality assurance
       Identified process   _____
       External standards   _____
       Internal standards   _____
       External benchmarks   _____
       Internal benchmarks   _____

Resources
Equipment
    Internal   _____
    External   _____
    Materials
    Internal   _____
    External   _____
    Skills
    Internal   _____
    External   _____
Contacts
    Internal   _____
    External   _____
    Project management tools
    Internal   _____
    External   _____
    Development tools
    Internal   _____
    External   _____
Facilities
    Internal   _____
    External   _____
    Logistics requirements   _____
Training requirements
    Internal   _____
    External   _____
Documentation requirements
    Internal   _____
    External   _____
Communications requirements
    Internal   _____
    External   _____

01VIABI INSTRUCTIONS FOR USING A VIABILITY CHECKLIST

General Instructions
- This checklist is only a framework for you to create your own 20 questions.

- There are two required questions in any situation:

  1. Is there funding available for a potential project?

  2. Are there measurable goals for a potential project?

- Each of these items will require its own set of questions based on the metaquestions (How?, Why?, When?, Where?, Who?, and What?) that lead to a "yes," "no," or "not applicable." From these questions, the list should be narrowed to 20 for the meeting with the project initiator.

- Do not expect to have acceptable set of questions on the first try.

- When presenting your questions it might effective to have a slide for each. The potential customer should focus on each question rather than on the 20 as a whole. It is more important to have a visual presentation rather you just asking each question.

- You might include very brief talking points on each slide such "Criteria for adequate funding."

Specific Instructions

Measurable goals: "Win the game" appears to be a measurable goal; however, does it mean the game must be won by more than one point? In the same manner, the goal of completing the project on time and on budget is not measurable. What must specifically be completed?

Acceptable assumptions: An assumption is a prediction that action or an event will be fulfilled. An example is "There will be potential risks, but they will all be overcome."

Acceptable constraints: A constraint is a limit, limitation, or parameter such as the duration or funds available for the project.

Identified deliverables: A deliverable is a measurable result, product, or service of the project.

Identified risks: A risk is event that will bring failure to the project.

Identified opportunities: An opportunity is a situation that can shorten the project's duration or lessen funding requirements.

Identified project impacts: An impact can be either short-term or long-term. When a risky long-term is forgotten such as the maintenance time required for a piece of hardware in a network in the field is ignore in the design of it. The cost can reduce any profits from the project.

Identified stakeholders: A stakeholder is potentially anyone in the organization, members of an external funding group, users, and interested government regulators.

Established project process: When there is no established project process, there is no management. There is firefighting. Would you want to do business with someone who cannot tell you how they are going to achieve your measurable goals?

Adequate duration: Duration should be defined as to the amount of working days available for the project. An absolute duration such things as weekends. One might speak to a six-month duration; however, what is the production time?

Criteria for time estimates: If you do not have measurable and object criteria for time estimates, the project will fail.

Schedule requirements: A schedule needs to consider in a project's duration its production-time and its wait-time. It is an allocation of activities with deadlines or milestones.

Acceptable deadlines: Acceptable deadlines are realistic. They can also be defined within either a pessimistic or an optimistic scenario.

Cost-benefit analysis: An IS cost-benefit analysis is required before any viability. Any questions should be formulated within in the context of the results.

ROI impacts: A Return on Investment is more than a financial saving. An ROI could also be an adequate security system that protects data and its loss to a cracker (thief) could not adequately be estimated.

Adequate available funding: If there is no available funding, the project is only speculation.

Budget requirements: A project budget is a formal structure that is based on changing cost estimates. A project budget is not a corporate annual budget that is based on headcount and activities.

Criteria for cost estimates: If you do not have measurable and object criteria for cost estimates, the project will fail.

Project authority adequate: A written document that establishes the parameters of authority for the project manager must completed prior to start of the project.

System infrastructure effects: The infrastructure is more that the visual components (hardware, software, and people). It includes the intangible tangibles: compatibility, interoperability, portability, and scalability.

Technology stability: Do you know of any potential technology that could impact the measurable goals of the project?

Quality control: Quality control is the definition component of a quality program. You need to know the potential impacts of internal and external objective and measurable standards (procedures) and benchmarks (performance level) on completing the project's goals.

Quality assurance: Quality control is the performance (the data gathering) component of a quality program. You need to know the potential uses of internal and external objective and measurable standards (procedures) and benchmarks (performance level) on completing the project's goals.

Resources: You need to have knowledge as to resource requirement types potentially required before any viability meeting. The knowledge should internal and external equipment requirements, materials, skills, contacts, system and development tools, facility requirements, and finally training and documentation needs. Why do you need all this data up front? You need to be able to judge as adequately as possible your capabilities to do the customer's stated measurable goals.

Training requirements: Training requirements need to consider the availability of internal and external classes. Will the training include hands-on situations? What is the learning curve scenario? What are the potential funding requirements? When is the training requirement to determine the critical path?

Documentation requirements: Documentation requirements have to consider if all or some of the documents are written. What kind of funding is needed? What type of documentation is required (technical, customer, or training)?

Communications requirements: Communications requirements have to consider the methods for get information to a person in an appropriate manner? Who gets what information must be defined. Do you give weekly reports to the customer using e-mail or do you give monthly presentations of project status? What the benefits and consequences of using e-mail? Consider that e-mails can be forwarded to people outside of the project's environment and sometimes be interpreted on an emotional level.

Example Questions

Below are 10 questions in the "yes-no" response format for the project viability process:

* Are there measurable project goals?
* Is there sufficient justification (cost-benefit analysis, customer relationship, or general market environment) to do this project been given?
* Is there sufficient funding?

- Does the present staff have the skills to achieve the defined activities or tasks?
- Can the goals be achieved in the expected duration (time)?
- Are the necessary management tools available and are there appropriate skilled personnel available?
- Have the implications for possible benchmarks and standards been considered?
- Is there a written statement of tactical responsibility?
- Are there critical impacts on the system's infrastructure?
- Have criteria of potential risks been established?

While some of the above questions might not be answered absolutely at a meeting on project viability, they should be answered with a high degree of probability. A "maybe" answer should turned into a "yes" or "no" prior to a definite start of a project.

02SCOPEF DATA TYPE/DATA REFINEMENT FOR A SCOPE PLAN

1. What are the measurable customer's goals and deliverables?

   _____

   _____

   _____

2. How will the goals be funded and budgeted?

   _____

   _____

   _____

3. What are the critical activities for achieving the critical goals?

   _____

   _____

   _____

4. What resources are critical for success?

   _____

   _____

   _____

5. What are the criteria for defining pessimistic, realistic, and optimistic estimates?

   _____

   _____

   _____

6. Have potential threats and opportunities been identified for schedule changes?

   _____

   _____

   _____

7. What activities or expected goals require training?

   _____

   _____

   _____

8. What are the criteria for documenting the project activities?

   _____

   _____

   _____

9. How should the project's scope definition be used to develop the schedule?

   _____

   _____

   _____

10. Where have delays been factored into the schedule?

    _____

    _____

    _____

11. How do cost estimates affect the schedule?

    _____

    _____

    _____

12. How do resource estimates affect the schedule?

    _____

    _____

    _____

13. Are there any internal or external procurement policies or standards that affect the schedule?

    _____

    _____

    _____

14. How is training to be accomplished?

    _____

    _____

    _____

15. How is documentation to be accomplished?

    _____

    _____

    _____

16. Who is to create the organizational structure that links responsibilities activities and deliverables?

    _____

    _____

    _____

17. What are the standards and benchmarks for the quality assurance and control program?

    _____

    _____

    _____

18. What are performance criteria for the quality control assurance program?

    _____

    _____

    _____

19. What is the necessary time for quality validation?

    _____

    _____

    _____

20. Who should involved in a customer review?

    _____

    _____

    _____

02SCOPEI INSTRUCTIONS FOR THE SCOPE DATA TYPE/DATA
REFINEMENT FORM

Basic Terms

When filling out the form there are five basic definitions used for consistency of responses:

The **Scope Plan** is the strategic view of the constraints and assumptions of the project as developed by the project team.

A **constraint** is a parameter, limitation or a boundary for the project plan.

An **assumption** is a prediction that something will be true.

A **scope definition** is a measurable goal that becomes general procedures with measurable constraints and viable assumptions.

Scope planning is defining the goals and performance expectations of your project goals in measurable terms and getting an agreement on them.

Warnings

- The space given on the form is not to be considered a constraint as to length of response.

- Each response on the form should either read "See attachment XXX." or "No response is required."

- Each attachment needs a clear identifier so each can be associated correctly with the main form.

- Each response needs three estimate scenarios: pessimistic, realistic, and optimistic. The criteria for each scenario must also be given.

- Each question must be answer in the context of who, what, where, why, when, and how. For example, the last question on the form has five variants that need to be considered in the completed response:

- How should you manage a customer review?

- Why should there be a customer review?

- When should you hold a customer review?

- Where should you hold a customer review?

- What are the assumptions and constraints for holding a customer review?

Specific Instructions

1. Goals and deliverables are data types. The actual customer goals and deliverables are data.

2. Is the funding in weekly, monthly, or quarterly increments?

3. A critical path in the minimum amount activities that can achieved in the least time to do the defined measurable goals that are necessary, not optional or nice.

4. Critical resources are the minimal required resources as defined in a pessimistic scenario.

5. These criteria need to be based on objective sources (standards and performance benchmarks) and defined prior to writing estimates.

6. A threat is not necessarily a risk. A risk produces project failure. An opportunity can be used to reduce a project's duration or funding.

7. Training includes hands-on learning curves. The lack of defining the informal training may cause a bigger risk than the defined training events.

8. Documentation requirements because of project goals should be considered in the manner as the training requirements. A document on a software application or utility should not be written without input from the programmers.

9. The scope plan should include event durations, milestones, and so forth. These should be used to create a visual schedule.

10. Factored delays are contingencies not padding.

11. A cost estimate may generate a budget item. When the funding is available does affect the schedule.

12. A resource estimate may generate a budget item. When the resource is available does affect the schedule.

13. Corporate procurement policies and procedures that potentially affect the scope of the project need to be explained.

14. Training may be internal, external, hands-on, formal, or informal. There might be online courses, classroom experiences, text, or seminars.

15. Documentation can by a writing group, technical personnel, or purchased out-of-the-box.

16. The "who" of this question are not necessarily an individual, but a team.

17. There must be identified procedural standards and performance benchmarks for any quality program. The standards can be external (organizations or companies) and internal (corporate, IS, or project team developed).

18. Quality assurance's performance criteria should be based on objective criteria from the standards and benchmarks collected in response to question 17.

19. Validation should be defined at the beginning of the project, not as an afterthought.

20. The response may be more an emotional one than a rational one. Begin by defining what you mean by a customer review.

A Potential Scope Plan Structure

The following is a potential 10-part Scope Plan:

1. Scope definition
2. Project assumptions and constraints
3. Authority statement
4. Organizational structure with responsibility links
5. Baseline plan
6. Estimate criteria
7. Communication program
8. Risk management parameters
9. Training program
10. Documentation program

Support Documents Used with the Scope Plan

Business Affiliate Plan
Business Justification
Commercial Specification
Content Agreement
Customer Documentation Strategy
Design and Development Plan

Field Introduction Requirements
Initial Budget Estimates
Initial Funding Requirements
Market Analysis Report
Project Cost Updates
Project Proposal
Project Specification
Project Support Plan
Quality Plan
Statement of Work (SOW)
Third-Party Market Agreement
Third-Party Service Plan
Training Strategy
Trial (Beta) Strategy

03ACTF PROJECT TASK IDENTIFICATION

TASK IDENTIFICATION CHECKLIST _____

Organization _____

Source: _____

_____

_____

Attachment ID: _____

Date: _____   Estimate Type:_____

Critical ( )   Pessimistic ( )
Optional ( )   Realistic ( )
Standard ( )   Optimistic ( )

1. Task measurable goals and deliverables

2. Task assumptions and constraints

3. Criteria for resource requirements

4. Critical tasks and their critical activities

5. Skills criteria

6. Contingency criteria and requirements

7. Funding requirements

8. Communications requirements
9. Procurement policy and procedural requirements
10. Quality control and verification requirements
11. Training requirements
12. Documentation requirements
13. Risk management concerns
14. Miscellaneous Comments

03ACTI INSTRUCTIONS FOR PROJECT TASK IDENTIFICATION

Essential Terms

- *An* activity is an *event* with a start- and finish-date that uses resources such designing a section of an application.
- A *task* is a collection of activities such as designing all the sections of an application.
- A *deliverable* is the designed application or product.
- A *milestone* or *gate* is the actual start- and finish-dates of the designing task for the application or product.
- The rational basis for how, why, when, where, who, and what is defined by *assumptions* and *constraints. Thus, an assumption or a constraint can have up to six basic components.*

Warnings

- Each response to the form ID should read "See attachment XXX."
- Each attachment needs a clear identifier so each can be associated correctly with the main form.
- Each task needs three estimate scenarios: pessimistic, realistic, and optimistic. The criteria for each scenario must also be given.
- Each response must be answered in the context of who, what, where, why, when, and how. For example, the following are six variants that need to be considered in completing a potential response:

  1. Who is responsible for defining critical task
  2. How should a critical task be defined?

3. Why should a given task be defined as critical?

4. When should a given task be critical?

5. Where should a critical path be done?

6. What are the assumptions and constraints for a critical path?

General Instructions

- Use one form for each task.
- Identify tasks based on the statement of work.
- Each task needs a set of activity assumptions and constraints.
- The result of a task must be measurable.
- Consider tasks needed for a deliverable and then the activities required for a given task.
- You should objective criteria for task identification. The essential sources are standards and benchmarks. There need to be consistency for the estimates.
- The checklist is an outline for an example Activity Plan organization is given. Each "chapter" should be considered in developing task identification responses.
- Do an analysis of what data are required by milestone or gate.
- Include start- and end-dates.
- Identify each task's requirement for resources, that is, cost, time, skills, hardware, and software. This means you need estimates and their criteria.
- Define all estimates in three scenarios: pessimistic, realistic (most likely), and optimistic.
- A simple format for essential data for a task is as follows:

Estimate	Optimistic	Realistic	Pessimistic
Cost	_____	_____	_____
Time	_____	_____	_____
Equipment	_____	_____	_____
Material	_____	_____	_____
Skill	_____	_____	_____

For the last three estimates, in the blanks give attachment ID.

Specific Instructions

1. The measurable goals of a task need to reflect the defined goals of the project found in the Scope Plan.

2. Use the Scope Plan to assist you in defining the assumptions and constraints for tasks. You cannot say "not applicable" for this requirement. All tasks have assumptions and constraints.

3. Define resources as critical, standard, or optional. A brief justification should be given for each task.

4. A critical task should be defined only when there is objective supporting evidence such as the need for a design phase a new piece of hardware or software. Identify tasks that might be needed when a situation is worse than pessimistic. This means the critical path breaks down.

5. Skills criteria should determine the resource requirement, not headcount. For example, you might say for an optimistic scenario that a network security technician with more than five years experience could do the task in one week. For a realistic scenario, a network security technician with two to four years experience could do the task in less than one month. For a pessimistic scenario, a network security technician with less than one year of experience might do the task in three months.

6. There must be a change mechanism or requirement for each task sequence. Include in the contingency section of the response. Informal padding should not be done. State the range of your needs and the criteria for a range.

7. State when funding is required. Do say that all the funding must be up front. Funding requirements should be given in monthly increments.

8. Communication requirements how correct information is to get from you to other people in the correct amount of time. You might give task updates verbal or written to the project team once a month or after task X is completed. Another example, you will e-mail to keep your team informed.

9. The tasks that are required for resource availability need to be defined. Identify appropriate corporate procurement policy by task. Identify any special requirements the project manager has to administer.

10. Identify quality control procedures by task. Give applicable procedural standards and performance benchmarks.

11. Identify the criteria for defining the training requirements for tasks. Include data on both formal and informal training, especially hands-on experience requirements and learning curve impacts.

12. There needs to be some activities for administrative documentation as well as documentation that might be used by the training and documentation groups.

13. Discuss potential risks and solution procedures. Risk particularly happen when a pessimistic scenario breaks down. Padded cost and time estimates are two of the three major reasons for project failure.

14. Criteria need to define the policy activities, the project administrative activities, and the work activities. An example of policy, an operational manager does not discuss privately with a customer about making changes. Any change needs to go through the project manager and documented.

Task and Activity Sequence Assistance

1. The first step in sequencing is to use the critical path method (CPM). All sequencing must resolve the critical activities and their shortest time line.

2. Do not confuse task or activity sequencing with scheduling. The schedule is a formal document that includes the tasks and the amount of time that the tasks require to be completed.

3. Identify the criteria for task and activity sequence.

4. Establish sequences based on defined deliverables.

5. Determine resource availability effects on sequences.

6. Consider the budgetary cycle impacts on sequences.

7. Consider documentation requirements and their impacts on sequences.

8. Consider training requirements and their impacts on sequences.

9. Determine the procurement policies that affect sequences.

10. Identify quality control procedures that might impact sequences.

11. Give the necessary links for the various sequences.

04RESF RESOURCE PLAN CHECKLIST

RESOURCE DEFINTION_____Type_____

Source: _____

_____

_____

Date: _____   Estimate Type:
                        Critical ( )   Pessimistic ( )
                        Optional ( )   Realistic ( )
                        Standard ( )   Optimistic ( )

Resource Description:
Hardware ( ) Software ( ) Skill ( ) Support ( )
Consultant ( )
available ( ) not available ( )/source

_____

Measurable Objectives:

_____

_____

Training required ( ) If checked, describe. _____

_____

_____

Documentation required ( ) If checked, describe.

_____

_____

_____

Time Estimates with Measurable Criteria:

_____

_____

_____

Cost Estimates with Measurable Criteria:

_____

_____

_____

Dependencies: *Description*
Events: _____

_____

Hardware: _____
Software: _____
Skills: _____
Support: _____
Consultant: _____
Training: _____
Learning Curve: _____
Documentation: _____
Timing: _____

Standards: _____

Benchmarks: _____

Performance Level: _____

Contingency: _____

_____

Quality Control:
Effectiveness: _____

_____

Efficiency: _____

_____

Variances: _____

_____

Risk Analysis: _____

_____

_____

_____

_____

Special Issues: _____

_____

_____

_____

04RESI INSTRUCTIONS FOR THE RESOURCE PLAN CHECKLIST

Key Definitions

A **resource** is anything that supports the project. This includes in general terms money, skills, materials, time, facilities, and equipment.

An **estimate** is a guess based on opinion or a forecast based on experience.

An **assumption** is a prediction that an action or an event will be true.

A **baseline plan** is the initial approved measurable point from which any deviations will be determined using standards and benchmarks.

A **benchmark** is specific measurable technical level of excellence.

Contingency is the rational preparation for change. It should be used instead of padding.

A **critical activity** is an activity that if not completed means project failure.

Dependency means that a resource has to be available before a task can be started or completed.

An **objective** (resource) is a set of measurable goals to have a resource that if not available produces critical results.

An **optimistic estimate** is an assumption that holds everything will go as planned.

Padding is an informal action (adding time or cost to an estimate) that should not take place. Any such estimates should be formalized as a contingency.

Performance is the measurable level of action to achieve a measurable project goal. It is the act or level of work demonstrated and judged based on an identified skill level (beginner, adequate, or expert).

A **pessimistic estimate** is an assumption is that if something will go wrong, it will.

A **realistic estimate** is an assumption is there will probably be a few difficulties, but with compromise, the difficulties will be overcome.

Skill level is used to identify production (resource) requirements rather than using headcount.

A **standard** is usually external and an industry-accepted document for achieving quality for the one or more of the project-defined expected goals. It is a primary resource.

Variance is any deviation from the planned work whether it is costs, time, or resources. It is used to specific pessimistic and optimistic cost, time, and resource requirement estimates.

General Instructions

- Cost and time estimates for resource should included the following five situations:
  1. Resource descriptions
  2. Links
  3. Impacts
  4. Usage criteria
  5. Change requirements

- You should identify not only resources for operational and administrative activities, but also their utilization and availability constraints and assumptions.

- You should identify any resource based on required skill level rather than by a headcount. You need three skill resource definitions for pessimistic, realistic, and optimistic.

- When not included specifically in the checklist, you need to consider the why, what, where, when, and how of any response.

- You should give measurable for critical resources.

- You should state measurable criteria for estimating resources.

- You need to list measurable criteria for strategic, tactical, and operational resources.

- You need to state measurable criteria for any training or documentation requirements for the use of resources.

- You should list the measurable criteria for any potential risk that may impact resource acquisition.

- You give potential impacts of the availability of resources on the project's success.

- When required you need to note quality control requirements?

- When there is no applicability to a given answer on the checklist, state "There is no applicability."
- You should relate resources to cost, time, and activity estimates.
- You should relate the project scope definitions resource estimates.
- You should show any critical resource relationships.
- You should not any critical effects of the cost parameters on resource estimates.
- You should give the impacts of departmental milestones on the resource estimates.
- You should give a control system to manage resources and any changes.
- You should identify when possible procurement policies which need to be followed.
- You should not use an available resource to defined activities unless it critical to project goals.

Resource Identification Process

Before filling out the checklist, should do the following steps:

1. Make a list, as specific as possible, of required resources.
2. Identify mandatory resources.
3. Identify resources as belonging to a pessimistic, an optimistic, or a realistic scenario.
4. Identify resources that belong to a contingency plan (based on a pessimistic scenario).
5. Group resources by project phase — planning, designing, developing, testing, or implementing.
6. Order the resources by priority — you need to define what you mean by priority.
7. Group resources by users — can be by administrative unit or individual.
8. Group resources by impact — this means as mandatory or optional such as the resource has to be available before X activity or task.
9. Group resources by availability — full-time, part-time, have to buy, have to rent, and so forth.
10. List resources by training requirements.

WARNING

All criteria (standards, benchmarks, and goals) and skills should be measurable. You would not have a resource skill definition such as, "An XML programmer is required." What are the measurable deliverables from the programmer to achieve a specific project goal?

Specific Instructions

- Each resource requires three forms for each of these scenarios: pessimistic, realistic, and optimistic.

- Internal source includes responsible estimator, title, phone number, organization unit, e-mail address, and any other special personal identifiers

- External source should include all internal source data plus company address, and the name of the responsible company representative for the project.

- Date should be in the form of mm/dd/yy.

- Estimate type should include explanation of critical or optional in the last section of the form, special issues.

- Resource description should be included as an attachment with the form. A description should be written in the content of the key definitions given in these instructions. For example, a resource description for a piece hardware would include company name (part number), general use name, when required in the project, who is to use it, when and where is it to be used, what project goal is it for, present availability, procurement requirements, a permanent acquisition or a temporary lease, duration of use, and skill level requirements for use.

- Objectives should include the associated project goal. When appropriate, you should give related procedural standards and performance benchmarks, which justify the requirement of the resource.

- The training description should include availability, why required, what is the training to achieve, when and duration of the training, and where the training to be given. The names of the students should also be given as an attachment.

- The documentation description must include availability, why required, what is the documentation to achieve when is it to be used, and who needs the documentation.

- Time estimates are one of the three major reasons for project failure. The description used measurable and precise. Any estimate should take in consideration all these instructions.

- Cost estimates have the same impacts as time estimates.

- A dependency is a must requirement before a given project event (task) can be started or completed. For example, a person must acquire a certain level of knowledge before one can begin the task (learning curve and training).

- The standard description should include name, organizational source, date, version number, where it can be located (may be a URL), pertinent paragraph numbers, and relevant quality control considerations.

- The benchmark description should be similar to the standard description.

- The performance description should be measurable and should include the source for the performance level.

- Contingency is not padding. A contingency is a factor based on pessimistic or optimistic measurable criteria.

- Quality control descriptions should include information that can be integrated into a quality control program.

- The risk analysis description should be based on the estimate type of the form: pessimistic, realistic, or optimistic.

- The special issue should include any special considerations to clarify any prior descriptions on the form.

05TIMEF TIME ESTIMATES CHECKLIST

ATTACHMENTS

Time estimates by scenario
     Pessimistic   _____
     Realistic   _____
     Optimistic   _____
Criteria by scenario
     Pessimistic   _____
     Realistic   _____
     Optimistic   _____
Impacts by scenarios

      Pessimistic   _____

      Realistic   _____

      Optimistic   _____

Estimates by project goals   _____

Source ID   _____

Critical estimates

      Procurement tasks   _____

      Skills development   _____

      Resource tasks   _____

      Material gathering   _____

      Support tasks   _____

      Training tasks   _____

      Documentation tasks   _____

      Production tasks

            Planning   _____

            Design   _____

            Development   _____

            Testing   _____

Defined assumptions used   _____

Defined constraints used   _____

Deliverables accounted for   _____

Adequate duration   _____

Schedule requirements used   _____

Deadline criteria   _____

Quality

      Control   _____

      Assurance   _____

      Validation   _____

      Field testing   _____

Resource procurements

      Equipment

            Internal   _____

            External   _____

      Materials

            Internal   _____

            External   _____

      Skills

            Internal   _____

            External   _____

Project management tools
    Internal   _____
    External   _____
Development tools
    Internal   _____
    External   _____
Facilities
    Internal   _____
    External   _____
Logistics
    Internal   _____
    External   _____
Training requirements
    Internal   _____
    External   _____
Documentation requirements
    Internal   _____
    External   _____
Communications requirements
    Internal   _____
    External   _____
Risk management   _____
Project administration   _____

SPECIAL TIME ESTIMATE CRITERIA
Duration
    Production-time   _____
    Wait-time   _____
    Calendar days   _____
    Period/Effort   _____
Dependency
    end-start   _____
    start-end   _____
    start-start   _____
    lag time   _____
    lead time   _____
    slack time   _____
Trade-off considerations
    Part time staff   _____

Full time staff   _____

Other   _____

Special variants noted   _____

Consistency to:

    Scope Plan   _____

    Activity Plan   _____

    Resource Plan   _____

Manager's approval   _____

05TIMEI INSTRUCTIONS FOR THE TIME ESTIMATES CHECKLIST

This checklist assists the project team in the writing the Project Activity Plan, the Project Schedule and the Project Budget. It is used by each operational manager to do these documents at a group level or departmental level.

Time estimates by scenario: All project time estimates must be given in three forms: pessimistic, realistic, and optimistic. Actual format instructions come from the project team. The estimates should reflect items given in this checklist. A confidence level should be included with each estimate.

Criteria by scenario: There should be objective data to support the three types of estimates. The sources for the criteria include standards, benchmarks, historical records, or project team requirements.

Impacts by scenario: There should be explanations for each of the estimate types. For example, the estimate is pessimistic because no one is immediately available at this time with the skill level to do the task in less than three months. Another example is if the pessimistic estimate happens, then "X" risk may happen by affecting other estimates.

Estimates by project goals: Estimates should be linked to the projects goals as found in the Project Scope Plan.

Source ID: Identify the person responsible for writing the time estimates, including title, e-mail address, and telephone number. If an external source, also include company information.

Critical estimates: For the listed items give the justifications for being designated critical.

Defined assumptions: Use the assumptions from the Scope Plan to develop estimates.

Defined constraints: Use the constraints from the Scope Plan to develop estimates.

Deliverables: Give links to project deliverables for each estimate.

Adequate duration: Give the criteria for task duration that includes both production- and wait-times.

Schedule requirements: Use the Project Schedule requirements as defined by the project team.

Deadline criteria: Use deadline criteria as defined by the project team that is based on the Scope Plan.

Quality: Give any possible estimates that you consider relevant to the listed areas that might be required for product validation or field testing. Justifications should be included such as reference to a standard or benchmark.

Resource procurements: If a resource (hardware, software, skill, or support materials) has to be acquired from an external source, give estimates for the procurement tasks such as negotiation and administrative times.

Risk management: Consider if a pessimistic scenario breaks down, the possible time required for correcting.

Project administration: Based on the project team requirements, give estimates. In addition, consider time estimates for giving status reports to operational team by either e-mail or status presentations.

SPECIAL TIME ESTIMATE CRITERIA

Each of the following items is of a technical nature to assist you in writing a time estimate:

Duration

Production-time: Actual days of work.

Wait-time: Actual days when work is not being done such as weekends and holidays.

Calendar days: Use the Gregorian calendar.

Period/Effort: A period is an amount of time, while an effort is the amount of work to complete a task.

Dependency:

End-start: It means that an activity or task must end before another can start.

Start-end: It means that an activity or task must begin before another activity or task can end.

Start-start: It means that one activity or task must start before another.

Lag time: It is the time between two activities or tasks because of the nature of the activities.

Lead time: It is the overlapping time of two activities or tasks.

Slack time: It is the difference between earliest and latest (start or finish) times for an activity or a task.

Trade-off considerations:
Part time staff: State such as one hour per day or once a week. Justify the use of a part time staff over the use of a full time.

Full time staff: Give impacts of having full time over part time. Justify the use of a full time staff over the use of a part time.

Other: Identify if there is a need for a consultant or any other outside staff.

Special variants: Give any additional information that might assist the project team in its responsibilities and minimize further discussions.

Consistency to: There should be links in the justifications or impacts to the listed documents.

Scope Plan: It is the strategic view of the constraints and assumptions of the project as developed by the project team.

Activity Plan: It is a set of definitions for efforts required to achieve measurable results. At the operational level, you consider activities; while at the project level, you consider tasks.

Resource Plan: It establishes support requirements for a project as to costs, availability, start-date and end-date (length of time for use plus duration), and technical specifications.

Manager's approval: The manager should be of an appropriate management authority to agree to the time estimate.

06SCHF CHECKLIST FOR CREATING A PROJECT SCHEDULE

Scenarios for each task:
      Pessimistic   _____
      Realistic   _____
      Optimistic   _____
Critical path   _____
Duration
      Production-time   _____
      Wait-time   _____
      Lag time   _____
      Lead time   _____
Dependencies
      Start-end   _____
      Start-start   _____
      End-start   _____

Slack time   _____

Calendar structure   _____

Sequence integration

    Tasks   _____

    Resources   _____

    Spending   _____

    Procurement   _____

    Training   _____

    Documentation   _____

Links to:

    Resources   _____

    Skills   _____

    responsible people   _____

    Project Scope Plan

        Measurable goals   _____

        Assumptions   _____

        Constraints   _____

    Design and Development Plan   _____

    Activity Plan   _____

    Resource Plan   _____

    Task relationships   _____

Major milestones

    Deliverables

        Milestones (Gates)   _____

        Deadlines   _____

    Communications milestones   _____

    Logistics

        Location   _____

        Milestones   _____

    Reviews   _____

    Quality events

        Control   _____

        Assurance   _____

    Budget   _____

    Vendor   _____

    Status presentations   _____

Schedule characteristics

    Readable   _____

    Usable   _____

    Reliable   _____

Consistent _____
Coherent _____
Manageable level of details _____
24X7 mode used _____
Resource leveling _____
Aligned _____
Graphics to highlight events
    Colors _____
    Icons _____
    Note indicators _____
    Company requirements _____
    Customer requirements _____
    Gantt chart requirements _____
Estimates vs. Actual Report _____

06SCHI INSTRUCTIONS FOR A PROJECT SCHEDULE CHECKLIST

This checklist is used to assist the project team to create the Project Schedule. It is to by used by each operational manager to do a schedule at a group level or departmental level.

> When the word "activity" is used, the reference is at the operational level, while "task" is used in reference to the Project Schedule. When "event" is used, it is in reference to a point in time such as the start date for an activity or task or for a milestone.

The core question for the design, development, and implementation of any schedule is "What is the most logical method of presenting integration tasks based on reliable estimates with a timeline so that it communicates clearly the measurable project goals?" The essential principle in responding to this question or these instruction is keep it simple.

The Project Schedule needs to be approved prior to refining the cost estimates and developing the Project Budget.

Task by scenario: The task level detail used must be manageable in that the Schedule has to be readable, useful, and reliable. Any detail must be given in three forms: pessimistic, realistic, and optimistic. This means if you have a start-end block, then must have three sets of dates. The ordering of the scenario is a local issue; however, the ordering of the scenarios must be consistent throughout the Schedule and departmental schedules. Another possibility is to have three separate schedules when using a simple linear graphic.

Critical path: A path is critical when there is no available time for the slippage of the activity or task (no slack time). The critical path method (CPM) in its simplest form is selecting the "must" activities and tasks, doing them in the shortest possible amount of time, and covering the shortest duration. A critical task is a task that if not completed means project failure.

Duration: The schedule is the duration of the project. It is the total involved time of an activity or task that is production-time plus wait-time. A project's duration is the total number of calendar days involved from start to end including the project manager's activities in closing the project.

Production-time: Since a schedule should use the 24X7 mode, production-time at an activity level can be stated in hourly or daily increments.

Wait-time: It duration minus production-time.

Lag time: This is the time between two activities or tasks because of their natures.

Lead time: This is the overlapping time of two activities or tasks.

Dependencies: A dependency is an event. An event is a point in time such as the start or end of an activity or task.

Start-end: This dependency means that an event must begin before another can end.

Start-start: This dependency means that one event must start before another.

End-start: This dependency means that an event must end before another can start.

Slack time: It is the difference between earliest and latest (start or finish) times for an activity or task.

Calendar structure: A schedule must be related to the Gregorian calendar in contrast to using effort.

Sequence integration: The most important activity or task sequence is of course the critical path. All other sequences should be related to it.

Tasks or activities: Task sequences are used at the Project Schedule level, while activities are used at the operational level.

Resources: Use the icons as determined by the project team plus a note indicator. The icon is a visual clue, while the note indicator permits text to be placed in a supplemental document such as details from the

Resource Plan. The may be a number of icons such as for critical hardware, software, materials, and skills.

Spending: As resources.

Procurement: As resources.

Training: As resources.

Documentation: As resources.

Links to: Use note indications and a special link icon as determined by the project team.

Resources: The resources here are the tactical ones such as hardware, software, and support materials (do not forget the pencils and paper).

Skills: The link must reference the skill type and its level to a person.

Responsible people: These group of people includes the customer representative, corporate manager for the project, the project manager, the project team, the operational managers, and consultants.

Project Scope Plan: It is the strategic view of the constraints and assumptions of the project as developed by the project team.

Measurable goals: These goals are from the Scope Plan.

Assumptions: They are predictions that something will be true, an event that ensures project success.

Constraints: They are parameters, limitations or boundaries for the project.

Design and Development Plan: It drives the project Integration Plan that captures all major design and development deliverables and milestones for management tracking and reporting.

Activity Plan: At the operational level, an activity plan is a set of definitions. A definition includes the activity's constraints from the Scope Plan. At the schedule level, the definitions are for tasks.

Resource Plan: This is the source document for identifying all the assumptions and constraints for the use of all the resources.

Task relationships: Relationships can be either between different organizations or within one organization.

Major milestones: Use the icons defined by the project team.

Deliverables: They are clearly defined project results, products, or services. They are outcomes.

Milestones (Gates): A milestone is a clearly defined date of start or 100 percent completion. A gate is another term for milestone or a major project event.

Deadlines: They are absolute dates. They are the critical sequence dependencies.

Communications milestones: They are the critical points in the process of getting the correct information to the correct location at the correct time. Note indicators should be used to reflect the specifics of the event such as a project management review. It is a regularly scheduled performance review.

Logistics: It is the process of getting the correct resource to the correct location at the correct time.

Reviews: All dates or events for management and technical reviews should be noted.

Quality events: The schedule quality events should be in two sequences. The control sequence includes the events for gathering and distributing information for or about the project. The assurance sequence includes the events for validation and testing based on performance.

Budget: Identify critical funding or spending milestones based on the finalized budget. This possible is the final act to be completed in the Project Schedule, beyond updates.

Vendor: A vendor has a product, while a consultant has information or services.

Status presentations: These include customer, upper level management, and team.

Schedule characteristics: These characteristics may be abstract; thus, agreement as to meanings should be by consensus of the project team.

Readable: The level of detail should not be so broad that an event cannot be identified easily.

Usable: The schedule should be so useful that is the basis for status presentations.

Reliable: The time estimates have to be valid.

Consistent: The use of icons and colors should bee the same whether the Project Schedule or the operational schedules.

Coherent: Events and task sequences should be synchronized.

Manageable level of details: Details at the Project Schedule level should be tasks, while at the operational level the details are based on activities.

24X7 mode used: The Schedule should be given in a 24X7 mode because some of the logistic events may occur at any time. In addition, critical tasks such as customer presentations may be identified in hours rather than a day.

Resource leveling: It is a technique to smooth out peaks and valleys for the use of resources.

Aligned: Alignment is another form of leveling except absolute dates are used.

Graphics to highlight events: Graphic standards are determined by the project team. However, red and green should only be used to highlight a negative or positive situation.

Colors: As determined by the project team. Do not use red or green except to highlight significant negative and positive events.

Icons: As determined by the project team. Icons are excellent to distinguish between types of links.

Note indicators: As determined by the project team.

Company requirements: Based on company policy or standard for a schedule's format.

Customer requirements: A special schedule might be done based on the customer's specified requirements. The requirements are a measurable goal of the project.

Gantt chart requirements: A Gantt chart is a visual presentation, a horizontal bar chart, of activities or tasks against time. A histogram is the opposite of a Gantt because vertical bars are used to represent values.

Estimates vs. Actual Report: This report should be updated at milestones and prior to any review briefing with the customer or upper level management.

07COSTF COST ESTIMATES CHECKLIST

ATTACHMENTS

Cost estimates by scenario
    Pessimistic   _____
    Realistic   _____
    Optimistic   _____
Criteria by scenario
    Pessimistic   _____
    Realistic   _____
    Optimistic   _____
Impacts by scenarios
    Pessimistic   _____
    Realistic   _____
    Optimistic   _____
Estimates by project goals   _____
Source ID   _____
Critical path estimates
    Procurement

Hardware _____

Software _____

Consultants _____

Special materials _____

Skills

Training _____

Procurement _____

Internal Resources _____

Support tasks _____

Documentation tasks _____

Production tasks

Planning _____

Design _____

Development _____

Testing _____

Non-critical path estimates

Procurement

Hardware _____

Software _____

Consultants _____

Special materials _____

Skills

Training _____

Procurement _____

Internal Resources _____

Support tasks _____

Documentation tasks _____

Production tasks

Planning _____

Design _____

Development _____

Testing _____

Defined assumptions used _____

Defined constraints used _____

Deliverables accounted for _____

Budget requirements used _____

Deadline criteria _____

Time estimates inputs _____

Quality
    Control   _____
    Assurance   _____
    Validation   _____
    Field testing   _____
Resource cost totals
    Equipment
        Internal   _____
        External   _____
    Materials
        Internal   _____
        External   _____
    Skills
        Internal   _____
        External   _____
        Approx. headcount _____
    Project management tools
        Internal   _____
        External   _____
    Development tools
        Internal   _____
        External   _____
    Facilities
        Internal   _____
        External   _____
    Logistics
        Internal   _____
        External   _____
Training cost totals
        Internal   _____
        External   _____
Documentation cost totals
        Internal   _____
        External   _____
Communications cost totals
        Internal   _____
        External   _____
Travel   _____

Risk management   _____
Project administration   _____

SPECIAL COST ESTIMATE CRITERIA

Links to time estimates   _____
Incremental spending periods
       One time   _____
       Monthly   _____
       Quarterly   _____
Vendor pricing
       Fixed   _____
       Variants from fixed   _____
Dependency
       Project goals   _____
       Project milestones   _____
       Task milestones   _____
       Learning curve   _____
       Special event   _____
Trade-off considerations
       Cost-benefit analysis
       Part time staff   _____
       Full time staff   _____
       Other   _____
Contingency Plan   _____
Special customer support   _____
Special variants noted   _____
Consistency to:
       Scope Plan   _____
       Activity Plan   _____
       Resource Plan   _____
       Project Schedule   _____
       Business Justification   _____
       Commercial Specification   _____
       Design/Development Plan   _____
       Market Analysis Report   _____
       Trial (Beta) Strategy   _____
       Request for Proposal   _____
Funding source approval   _____

07COSTI INSTRUCTIONS FOR A COST ESTIMATES CHECKLIST

This checklist is to produce consistency between the project requirements and the operational or functional areas. Ultimately these estimates are first compiled at the functional level and then consolidated as required in the Project Budget.

Cost estimates by scenario: All project cost estimates must be given in three forms: pessimistic, realistic, and optimistic. Actual format instructions come from the project team. All the estimates need to reflect items given in this checklist. A part of this task is to get a draft set of estimates. Second, these estimates are refined using outside assistance if necessary. Third, refine the estimates to determine if they are affordable for the customer. As a part of the refinements, a confidence level should be stated for each one.

Criteria by scenario: There should be objective data to support the three types of estimates. The sources for the criteria include time estimates, resource estimates, corporate billing policy, standards, benchmarks, historical records, or project team requirements.

Impacts by scenarios: There should be explanations for each of the estimate types. For example, the estimate is pessimistic because no one is immediately available at this time with the skill level to do the task; thus, an outside source must be procured. Another example is if the pessimistic estimate happens, then "X" risk may happen.

Estimates by project goals: Estimates should be linked to the projects goals as found in the Project Scope.

Source ID: Identify the person responsible for writing the time estimates, including title, e-mail address, and telephone number. If an external source, also include company information.

Critical path estimates: For the items listed give the justifications for being designated critical.

Non-critical path estimates: For the items listed give the formulae and their sources plus relevant standards or benchmarks for estimates.

Defined assumptions: Use the assumptions from the Scope Plan to develop estimates.

Defined constraints: Use the constraints from the Scope Plan and the time and resource estimates to develop estimates.

Deliverables: Give links to project deliverables for each estimate.

Budget requirements: Use the Project Budget requirements as defined by the project team. Check for rules of aggregation of cost estimates.

Deadline criteria: Use deadline criteria as defined by the project team that is based on the Scope Plan. The estimates might be affected by milestones, such as spending must completed by "X" event.

Time estimates impact: There should be objective data to support any time estimate. If the duration of a realistic time estimate for a linked task is too short or too long for your function, what are the potential impacts? For example, if "X" training course is more than two weeks in length, there will serious impacts such as "Y."

Quality: Give any possible estimates that you consider relevant to the listed areas that might be required for product validation or field tests. Justifications should be included such as reference to standards or benchmarks.

Resource cost totals: If a resource (hardware, software, skill, or support materials) has to be acquired from an external source, give estimates for the procurement tasks such as negotiation that includes travel and direct administrative costs. Internal costs refer to having to budget costs to another corporate functional groups such as Training or Documentation.

Travel: Give costs as to airplane, hotel, meals, and car rental. Justify requirements based on data given earlier with this form.

Risk management: Consider if a pessimistic scenario breaks down, the possible costs required for correction.

Project administration: Based on the project team requirements, give estimates. In addition, consider cost estimates for giving status reports to operational team by either e-mail or status presentations. It is possible that all of these costs are indirect.

SPECIAL COST ESTIMATE CRITERIA

Links to time estimates: Define links as they relate to costs. In addition, give links as appropriate to the Project Schedule.

Incremental spending periods: You must give spending increments based on the Project Schedule. Quarterly can be defined by the project team as either a three-month period of the project's duration or as a calendar quarter.

Vendor pricing:

Fixed: Justify the reasons a price is fixed for such items as hardware or training courses. Determine if the vendor is "buying the job."

Variants from fixed: Give the justifications for cost for a lesser item and a better item. In addition, consider the cost impacts of not getting the product.

Dependency: When appropriate give the dependency requirements for the listed items. First example is that a goal must be completed before completed before spending is required. Second example is that spending must be done before a milestone or event can be started. Give the cost impacts if a learning curve shortens or lengthens.

Trade-off considerations:

Cost-benefit analysis: When appropriate work with the marketing group to do an analysis that serves as a standard for the estimate.

Part time staff: State such as one hour per day or once a week. Justify the part time effort.

Full time staff: Give impacts of having full time over part time. Justify the use of full time staff over part time.

Other: Identify if there is a need for a consultant.

Contingency Plan: Give justifications for including a contingency amount and the potential requirements. This plan formalizes padding.

Special customer support: Include the possible "hidden" costs for corporate training, include travel.

Special variants: Give any additional information that might assist the project team in its responsibilities and minimize further discussions.

Consistency to: The listed documents should be used to define the environment for all costs estimates. Cost estimates should not be finalized until the Project Schedule is completed.

Scope Plan: It has the strategic view of the constraints and assumptions of the project as developed by the project team.

Activity Plan: It has a set of definitions for efforts required to achieve measurable results. At the operational level, you consider activities; while at the project level, you consider tasks.

Resource Plan: It establishes support requirements for a project as to costs, availability, start-date and end-date (length of time for use plus duration), and technical specifications.

Project Schedule: It formalizes the time estimates within a calendar structure. It is an integration of sequencing tasks, resource planning, cost estimating, and time estimating.

Business Justification: It is the general rationale for making the financial investment.

Commercial Specification: It is an evolution of the Business Justification. It identifies the market need and gives adequate requirement and limitation data for the design and development group(s).

Design/Development Plan: It drives the project Integration Plan that captures all major design and development deliverables and milestones for management tracking and reporting.

Market Analysis Report: It documents and verifies market opportunities and justifies the features, services, and applications for the project goals.

Trial (Beta) Strategy: It identifies the software and hardware elements in the project that are a part of any trial.

Request for Proposal: Ensure there is a consistency between the requirements of the RFP and the vendor's response. Ensure that response adheres to the requirements of this checklist.

Funding source approval: The funding source or sources must give a written agreement to the cost estimates.

08BUDF CHECKLIST FOR PROJECT BUDGET ITEMS

Budget methodology   _____
Corporate budget requirements:
      Table of accounts   _____
      Item locations   _____
      Item aggregation   _____
      Spending increments   _____
      Input requirements   _____
      Reporting structure   _____
Reporting requirements   _____
Funding sources
      Customer   _____
      Internal (IS)   _____
      Other   _____
Scenario type:
      Pessimistic   _____
      Realistic   _____
      Optimistic   _____
Link types to estimates by:
      Pessimistic   _____
      Realistic   _____
      Optimistic   _____
Milestones:
      Pessimistic   _____

Realistic   _____

Optimistic   _____

Links to project goals   _____

Links to deliverables   _____

Source ID   _____

Critical path items

    Procurement

        Hardware   _____

        Software   _____

        Consultants   _____

        Special materials   _____

    Skills

        Training   _____

        Procurement   _____

    Internal Resources   _____

    Support tasks   _____

    Documentation tasks   _____

    Production tasks

        Planning   _____

        Design   _____

        Development   _____

        Testing   _____

    Contingency   _____

Non-critical path items

    Procurement

        Hardware   _____

        Software   _____

        Consultants   _____

        Special materials   _____

    Skills

        Training   _____

        Procurement   _____

    Internal Resources   _____

    Support tasks   _____

    Documentation tasks   _____

    Production tasks

        Planning   _____

        Design   _____

        Development   _____

        Testing   _____

Links to assumptions   _____

Links to constraints   _____

Deadline impacts   _____

Time estimates inputs   _____

Quality items
- Control   _____
- Assurance   _____
- Validation   _____
- Field testing   _____

Resource items
- Equipment
    - Internal   _____
    - External   _____
- Materials
    - Internal   _____
    - External   _____
- Skills
    - Internal   _____
    - External   _____
    - Headcountequivalent   _____
- Project management tools
    - Internal   _____
    - External   _____
- Development tools
    - Internal   _____
    - External   _____
- Facilities
    - Internal   _____
    - External   _____
- Logistics
    - Internal   _____
    - External   _____

Training cost totals
- Internal   _____
- External   _____

Documentation cost totals
- Internal   _____
- External   _____

Communications cost totals
        Internal   _____
        External   _____
Travel
        Customer support   _____
        Training   _____
        Data gathering   _____
        Time requirements   _____
Vendors
        Functional   _____
        Goal   _____
        Deliverable   _____
        Time requirements   _____
        Payment requirements   _____
Dependency links
        Project goals   _____
        Project milestones   _____
        Task milestones   _____
        Learning curve   _____
        Special event   _____
Risk management   _____
Project administration   _____
Special variants noted   _____
Consistency to:
        Scope Plan   _____
        Activity Plan   _____
        Resource Plan   _____
        Project Schedule   _____
        Business Justification   _____
        Commercial Specification   _____
        Design/Development Plan   _____
        Baseline Plan   _____
Change management   _____
Update requirements   _____
Slippage rules   _____
Links to other budgets   _____
Funding source approval   _____
Estimates vs. Actual Report   _____

08BUDI INSTRUCTIONS FOR A PROJECT BUDGET CHECKLIST

This checklist may be used during the general estimating process; however, it cannot be completed until there is an approved Project Schedule. Time has cost.

There is one question for project budget design. It is "What method should I use so the project's budget is minimally impacted by the business budget cycle?" This checklist is the framework for answering this question.

There is a major assumption for project budget design. It is there should be three budgets: pessimistic, realistic, and optimistic. The realistic budget is the Project Budget. The other two budgets are the basis for change and contingency management.

A second assumption of the Project Budget is it is more than a list of budget items and the period when they will be funded or spent. There must be a set of support documents. Unfortunately, the project manager or an essential player might be loss from the project and there are no written parameters for then managing the budget.

Budget methodology: Use the "bottom-up" approach if budgeting can be done at the task level. However, if fund allocation is tight, then use the "top-down" approach to allocate funds at the functional level.

Corporate budget requirements: Before designing your own budget check for special corporate requirements and exceptions. In particular, check the listed items. If there is a requirement for the formal project budget to be a part of the corporate structure, ensure you can defined as many separate project budget items as possible from IS group budget items. You still need to create a set of informal project budget.

Reporting requirements: It is important to know corporate, customer, and project team requirements for information. These requirements affect the level of detail (table of accounts) for the budget.

Funding sources: When possible each source should be identified on a separate budget line. The other means such things as the Training group pays for customer training because of a marketing agreement.

Scenario type: Unfortunately, the basic attitude is that you have only one formal budget. Changes and updates can require a large amount of effort. By having three budgets up front, it saves administrative time during the project's duration.

Link types to estimates by: There needs to be a document that gives the source or responsible person for the cost estimates.

Milestones: The milestones help determine when there is to be funding and spending and the incremental amounts.

Links to project goals: Each budget item should have a link to one or more project goals as found in the Scope Plan.

Links to deliverables: When it is appropriate there should be links from budget items to deliverables, this includes training and documentation.

Source ID: Identify the person responsible for the budget item, including title, e-mail address, and telephone number. If an external source, also include company information.

Critical path items: The budget items for the critical path determine the fundamental design of the project budget. When there is no expenditure for a listed item, then $0.00 should be given on the checklist. It may be required to breakdown the list further such as production or testing hardware.

Contingency: It is the rational preparation for change. A contingency plan is the preparation for a pessimistic scenario or worse to become reality.

Non-critical path items: These items can be changed or even possible can be deleted without risk to the project. If this assumption is incorrect, then there needs to be a supporting document as to the possible amount of change or the impacts of deleting the budget item.

Links to assumptions: Use the assumptions in the Scope Plan and in cost estimates to determine a budget item and when amounts will be funded or spent.

Links to constraints: Use the constraints in the Scope Plan and in cost estimates to determine a budget item and when amounts will be funded or spent.

Deadline impacts: When amounts will be funded or spent are absolutely affected by deadlines since they are absolute dates or events.

Time estimates inputs: These inputs are used to determine when amounts for a given budget item is spent will be funded or spent. You never take a budget items amount and divide it by the monthly increments of the project's or a task's duration.

Quality items: Budget items for quality tasks should be divided by at least the four listed items. When there is only one line, it is difficult to determine impacts. In addition, the tasks by different groups and may be either internal or external.

Resource items: Amounts for various resource types should be detailed when possible especially if there is more than one funding source. When there is no expenditure for a listed item, then $0.00 should be given on the checklist.

Training: Integrate appropriate items in the Training Group's budget into the Project Budget. In addition, create special budget items for training done outside the Training Group.

Documentation: Integrate when appropriate in the related Documentation Group's budget items into the Project Budget. In addition, create special budget items for training done outside the Documentation Group.

Communications: Budget items, such, as cost to communicate with customer about the project's status would be here. Travel might be included here or under the travel budget item.

Travel: Budget items for travel should be broken down into a least the four categories.

Customer support: This item might be here or under communications. You should also include car rental, hotel, and meals.

Training: Use only if customer training is given in a project goal.

Data gathering: There may be a special requirement to go to a vendor's location. In this case the budget item can be here or located under budget.

Time requirements: If there is a direct cost, amounts should be defined. Indirect costs are never put in a budget. The costs for direct and indirect administrative efforts are one item in a standard budget. The corporate financial group usually states for a given head or a certain type and level, the budget factor is $175 per hour. This amount covers all the various administrative tasks and travel time say of a manager or programmer.

Vendors: The budget items can be broken down to function or deliverable. A budget support document should goal, time for funding or spending, and payment requirements.

Dependency links: When appropriate a document should be written that includes the appropriate listed items.

Risk management: There needs to be a budget item for potential risk corrections. This amount is a contingency, a known padding factor. An amount not spent might be moved to another budget item that has slippage if required when not spent during the month. A slippage is a form of risk.

Project administration: If there a corporate rule that certain administrative activities or tasks are consider direct then this budget item should in the project budget. For example, your costs for being a project manager might be here and your costs for being an IS manager would be given in the IS budget.

Special variants: There are always issues not covered in this checklist that need to be considered in the project budget.

Consistency to: The listed documents should be used to define the environment for all costs estimates. Cost estimates should not be finalized until the Project Schedule is completed.

Scope Plan: It is the strategic view of the constraints and assumptions of the project as developed by the project team.

Activity Plan: It is a set of definitions for efforts required to achieve measurable results. At the operational level, you consider activities; while at the project level, you consider tasks.

Resource Plan: It establishes support requirements for a project as to costs, availability, start-date and end-date (length of time for use plus duration), and technical specifications.

Project Schedule: It formalizes the time estimates within a calendar structure. It is an integration of sequencing tasks, resource planning, cost estimating, and time estimating.

Business Justification: It is the general rationale for making the financial investment.

Commercial Specification: It is an evolution of the Business Justification. It identifies the market need and gives adequate requirement and limitation data for the design and development group(s).

Design/Development Plan: It drives the project Integration Plan that captures all major design and development deliverables and milestones for management tracking and reporting.

Baseline Plan: It is the initial approved point from which any deviations will be determined using standards and benchmarks.

Change management: The procedure for changing the budget should be documented.

Update requirements: The procedure for updating the budget should be documented.

Slippage rules: It is when a budget item is overspent. The procedure for managing a slippage should be documented.

Links to other budgets: Rather than including the Training Group's budget items that directly affect the project, there can be a support document that gives these items.

Funding source approval: The funding source or sources must give written approval on all or part of the budget as is appropriate.

Estimates to Actual Report: It should be done after the financial group sends an update of funding and spending. No review briefing should be held with the customer until this report is completed. The exception to this is that budget issues are not on the agenda.

09QCF CHECKLIST FOR A QUALITY MANAGMENT PROGRAM

QUALITY CONTROL

Source ID   _____
Document Identification:
      Scope Plan   _____
      Activity Plan   _____
      Resource Plan   _____
      Schedule   _____
      Budget   _____
      Standards   _____
      Benchmarks   _____
      Verification   _____
      Testing   _____
      Time estimate criteria   _____
      Cost estimate criteria   _____
      Resource est. criteria   _____
      Skill criteria   _____
      Technical procedures   _____
      Technical policies   _____
      Procurement procedures   _____
      Procurement policies   _____
      Communications   _____
      ISO standards   _____
      PMI standards   _____
      Customer sat. criteria   _____
Critical path criteria   _____
Identify skill criteria:
      Pessimistic   _____
      Realistic   _____
      Optimistic   _____
Establish tasks criteria:
      Planning   _____
      Design   _____
      Development   _____
      Production   _____
      Testing   _____
Task sequencing criteria   _____
Determine reviews requirements:
      Time estimates   _____

Cost estimates _____

Resource estimates _____

Project adm. criteria _____

Assumptions:

Criteria _____

Validation criteria _____

Constraints:

Criteria _____

Validation criteria _____

Determine field test criteria _____

Identify training criteria:

Validation _____

Testing _____

Identify documentation criteria:

Validation _____

Testing _____

Identify Quality support tasks _____

Variances criteria:

Time _____

Cost _____

Resources _____

Variance reporting criteria _____

Risk management criteria _____

Specify random inspection criteria:

Equipment _____

Materials _____

Skills _____

Project management tools _____

Development tools _____

Facilities _____

Logistics _____

Training _____

Documentation _____

Communications _____

Specify audit criteria:

Equipment _____

Materials _____

Skills _____

Project management tools _____

Development tools _____

Facilities   _____
Logistics   _____
Training   _____
Documentation   _____
Communications   _____
Vendors:
    Assist writing RFPs   _____
    Gather performance history   _____
    Gather validation criteria   _____
    Gather testing criteria   _____
Dependency identification:
    Project goals   _____
    Project milestones   _____
    Task milestones   _____
    Learning curve   _____
    Special events   _____
Consistency determination criteria:
    Scope Plan   _____
    Activity Plan   _____
    Resource Plan   _____
    Project Schedule   _____
    Project Budget   _____
    Business Justification   _____
    Commercial Specification   _____
    Design/Development Plan   _____
    Baseline Plan   _____
    Field Introduction   _____
Gather change management criteria   _____
Identify update requirements   _____
Describe slippage rules   _____
Contingency Plan criteria   _____
Resource leveling assistance   _____
Gather logistics criteria   _____
Gather modeling data   _____
QUALITY ASSURANCE
Source ID   _____
Review viability responses   _____
Confirm project adm. criteria   _____

Analyze skills:
    Pessimistic   _____
    Realistic   _____
    Optimistic   _____
Validate document usage:
    Scope Plan   _____
    Activity Plan   _____
    Resource Plan   _____
    Schedule   _____
    Budget   _____
    Standards   _____
    Benchmarks   _____
    Verification   _____
    Testing   _____
    Time estimate criteria   _____
    Cost estimate criteria   _____
    Resource est. criteria   _____
    Skill criteria   _____
    Technical procedures   _____
    Technical policies   _____
    Procurement procedures _____
    Procurement policies   _____
    Communications   _____
    ISO standards   _____
    Customer sat. criteria   _____
Authenticate tasks criteria:
    Planning   _____
    Design   _____
    Development   _____
    Production   _____
    Testing   _____
Assist in field testing   _____
Validate training performance _____
Verify documentation:
    Customer   _____
    User   _____
    Technical (IS)   _____
    Reports   _____

Do Quality support tasks   _____

Validate and test assumptions   _____

Validate and test constraints   _____

Assist in reviews:

        Time estimates checklists   _____

        Cost estimates checklists   _____

        Resource estimates   _____

        Task ident. checklists   _____

        Task sequencing   _____

        Critical path   _____

        Contingency Plan   _____

Approve risk management criteria   _____

Do variance reports   _____

Perform random inspections:

        Identify variances and causes:

                Time   _____

                Cost   _____

                Resources   _____

        Equipment   _____

        Materials   _____

        Skills   _____

        Project management tools   _____

        Development tools   _____

        Facilities   _____

        Logistics   _____

        Training   _____

        Documentation   _____

        Communications   _____

Perform audits:

        Identify variances and causes:

                Time   _____

                Cost   _____

                Resources   _____

        Equipment   _____

        Materials   _____

        Skills   _____

        Project management tools   _____

        Development tools   _____

        Facilities   _____

Logistics _____

Training _____

Documentation _____

Communications _____

Project management process _____

IS procedures and process _____

Manufacturing _____

Other support groups _____

Vendors:

Review RFP responses _____

Analyze performance history _____

Confirm validation process _____

Confirm testing process _____

Confirm dependency usage:

Project goals _____

Project milestones _____

Task milestones _____

Learning curve _____

Special event _____

Consistency validation:

Scope Plan _____

Activity Plan _____

Resource Plan _____

Project Schedule _____

Project Budget _____

Business Justification _____

Commercial Specification _____

Design/Development Plan _____

Baseline Plan _____

Field Introduction _____

Validate change management process _____

Validate update process _____

Validate slippage usage _____

Do feedback reports _____

Assistance resource leveling _____

Analyze logistics criteria _____

Assist in model development _____

Validate and test deliverables _____

09QCI INSTRUCTIONS FOR A QUALITY MANAGEMENT PROGRAM CHECKLIST

Quality Management is the process that seeks to prevent risks and if a risk occurs minimizes it. The Quality Plan defines the tasks of Quality Management's two functions, Control and Assurance, in all phases of the project process.

It is the purpose of this checklist to assist in the writing of the plan.

Guiding principle for responding to this checklist is that Quality Control creates the map, while Quality Assurance drives a route based on the map.

This comprehensive checklist should be used to the level of detail that produces an effective and efficient Quality Management for the project.

QUALITY CONTROL: It is the quality management component, which considers the system or the development of a project's processes. It has tasks used to gather performance information requirements, that is standards and benchmarks.

Source ID: Identify the person responsible for the budget item, including title, e-mail address, and telephone number. If an external source, also include company information.

Document Identification: This task results in a distributed document that identifies the location of listed documents and the methods of acquisition. There should be brief descriptions of the relevance of documents to the project. Two optional project process document sets are the ISO and PMI standards. The International Organization for Standardization is a consortium that sets process standards in a variety of areas. The Project Management Institute is a professional organization that studies and promotes project management through its standards. The standards should be more than technical, they should include the requirements for stakeholder satisfaction (customer, management, and team); financial variances; and the impacts of innovation on the project and on the IS infrastructure as to interoperability, reliability, and scalability.

Critical path criteria: A critical project task means that if it is not completed there is a potential project failure. This task is to identify the criteria for meaning of critical. Second, the task is to assists in the design and development the critical path. Third, the task is to distribute the path criteria as required by the project team.

Identify skill criteria: The task is to gather information so there is consistency in the method of defining skills on three levels (pessimistic, realistic, and optimistic).

Establish tasks criteria: The task is to develop criteria that distinguish between a task and an activity for the Project Schedule for the listed project phases.

Task sequencing criteria: The task is to gather information to ensure that task sequencing is done in a consistent manner so project goals are completed.

Determine reviews requirements: The task is to gather objective criteria and any special customer, company, or project team requirements to ensure the three major types of estimates meet any relevant standards or benchmarks.

Project adm. criteria: The task is to define administrative criteria to ensure that the project process uses a systematic and sequential set of tasks to achieve a set of measurable and realistic goals. The results should include essential tasks of the project manager, the project team, and the operational managers. One of the project management techniques that needs to be considered in the development of criteria is the Program Evaluation and Review Technique (PERT). It combines statistics and network diagrams.

Assumptions: In general, they are predictions that something will be true, either an action or an event that ensures project success. First, this task assists in defining any criteria (pessimistic, realistic and optimistic). Second, this task establishes the criteria that are used to validate or test project components as to performances or results. Third, these assumptions and their validation requirements are organized into a document and distributed as required.

Constraints: In general, they are parameters, limitations, or boundaries for the project such as the Project Schedule or the Project Budget. First, this task assists in identifying any constraints (pessimistic, realistic and optimistic). Second, this task establishes the criteria that are used to validate or test if these constraints are being used in the project process. Third, these assumptions and their validation requirements are organized into a document and distributed as required.

Determine field test criteria: The task is to gather data for the Trial (Beta) Strategy that identifies the software and hardware elements in the project that are a part of any trial. Also the where, the when, the how, and by whom should be included in the strategy. This provides a clear identification of the testing requirements plus the extent of the resources and capabilities for a trial.

Identify training criteria: The task is to gather data for doing validation testing of defined project goals and results for formal and informal training. The task includes identifying required skill levels to training events.

Identify documentation criteria: The task is to gather data for doing validation testing of defined project goals and results for customer, user, and technical support documents. The task includes identifying document links to project goals.

Identify Quality support tasks: The task is to do any special tasks indirectly implied from the project goals or by the project team not given in this checklist.

Variances criteria: The task is to gather the criteria for determining normal and risk variances. A variance is any deviation from the planned work whether it is costs, time, or resources.

Variance reporting criteria: The task is to gather data on method for writing variance reports. Other data to be included would be when they should be completed, why they should be written, and for whom they should be given.

Risk management criteria: The task is to gather the benchmarks for determining risks and potential scenarios that foreshadow them. A risk is a performance error that can have a significant or disastrous impact on the success of a project or major activity. It is not just a problem. A scenario is a set of possibilities that could happen to cause a risk.

Specify random inspection criteria: The criteria are for an independent evaluation or test of a part of a listed project components by qualified personnel. Independent here means evaluation by either QA or an outside consultant. The criteria should be distributed as required by the project team.

Specify audit criteria: The criteria are for an independent evaluation or test of one of the listed project components by qualified personnel. Independent here means evaluation by either QA or an outside consultant. The criteria should be distributed as required by the project team.

Vendors:

Assist writing RFPs: The task is ensure a Request for Proposal is consistent with related project goals and milestones, technical performance requirements, quality process, skill level requirements, and competitive position.

Gather performance history: Performance as used here means there are objective data that demonstrates vendor can act at level of work required by the RFP.

Gather validation criteria: This task is to identify methods for validating information from vendors against project goals.

Gather testing criteria: This task is to identify methods for testing information from vendors against project goals.

Dependency identification: Dependency means that a task has to be completed before or after another one. For example, coding has to be completed before code testing can be completed. Less obvious is that a code test has to be written before code testing. A document should be a collection dependencies for at least the listed items and distributed in accordance with the project team's instructions.

Consistency determination criteria: The task is to identify the data links between the listed documents so that which is stated is the same sequentially through the documents.

Baseline Plan: This task is to define the initial approved point from which any deviations are determined using standards and benchmarks. This document or parts of it will be distributed as approved by the project team.

Field Introduction: The task is to assist in the writing in the Trial (Beta) Strategy.

Gather change management criteria: The task is to classify the parameters required to make changes to the project estimates in particular those that directly affect the Schedule and Budget as to who, what, why, when, where, and how.

Identify update requirements: The task is to describe the parameters required to make updates to the project estimates in particular those that directly affect the Schedule and Budget as to who, what, why, when, where, and how.

Describe slippage rules: The task is to define a potential schedule or budget slippage and how and when it should be reported. Budget slippage happens when a budget item is overspent. Time slippage is expected when you know about it before the due date, while is unexpected when you learn about the fact after the due date.

Contingency Plan criteria: This task is to prepare a document of potential causes and solutions using pessimistic scenarios or worse with the potential that they will become reality. In addition, the document includes identifies time and cost estimates that have a contingency value.

Resource leveling assistance: The task is to do leveling that is the technique of smoothing out peaks and valleys for the use of resources in a Project Schedule.

Gather logistics criteria: The criteria should ensure the logistics process gets the correct resource to the correct location at the correct time. The criteria should be published as required by the project team.

Gather modeling data: The task is to define the data requirements for doing models or simulations to ensure theoretically that process results as defined by required project goals can be validated prior to project completion. However, more preferable is validation before project development begins.

QUALITY ASSURANCE: The function is based on performance. It uses defined performance benchmarks to measure and evaluate project task performances. This component of quality management considers measurable deviations in performance during a project in a systematic manner. All tasks imply the need for measuring effects on IS interoperability, reliability, scalability, resource management (effectiveness and efficiency), and perhaps most importantly quality of performance.

Source ID: Same as QC instruction.

Review viability responses: The task is to assist the project manager in the responses from the project viability process before any review by upper level management.

Confirm project adm. criteria: The task is to validate the defined administrative criteria are being used to ensure that the project process is systematic and sequential to achieve the project's measurable goals. The validation includes the project administrative tasks of the project manager, the project team, and the operational managers. While this checklist does reflect the more specific tasks of the project management process, a broad set of project administration areas needs to be monitored and evaluated. The areas include planning, organizing, systematic processing for nontechnical areas (financial, communications, and change and risk management), and control management (resources, cost, and time).

Analyze skills: The task is to analyze the skill requirements and the demonstrated abilities of the person holding the skill.

Validate document usage: This task should use inspections and audit to determine if project stakeholders are adhering to criteria relevant to the project as found in the listed documents.

Authenticate tasks criteria: The task is to authenticate that tasks drive the project level process, while activities drive the operational level processes.

Assist in the field test: The task is to ensure the process in the Trial (Beta) Strategy is followed. In addition, the task includes when technical expertise is available to give support in the completion of the test.

Validate training performance: The task is to validate that formal and when possible informal training meet the project goals and that it produces the required skill levels to achieve realistic estimates.

Verify documentation: The task is to validate that the listed document types are written in accordance with project goals and requirements.

Do Quality support tasks: The task is to do any special tasks implied from the project goals not given in this checklist.

Validate and test assumptions: First, this task randomly validates and tests any critical assumptions. Second, this task validates the assumptions for validating or testing project components as to performances or results. Third, the results are organized into documents as required and distributed.

Validate and test constraints: First, this task validates and tests critical constraints. Second, this task determines how the criteria are being used in the project process. Third, the results are organized into documents and distributed as required.

Assist in reviews: For the listed items the task is for QA to have a review member that determines that estimates, tasks, and plans reflect the project goals as stated in the Scope Plan.

Critical path: This task is to assist in the review of the critical path plan. Second, this task is to report to the project team on negative and positive deviations from the criteria as to adherence to the critical path.

Contingency Plan: This task first gives assistance in reviewing the document. Second, it validates the need for a particular part of the plan to go into affect.

Approve risk management criteria: The task is to analyze the benchmarks for determining risks and potential scenarios that foreshadow them and determine if all goals have been covered. In addition, the task includes verifying the project process against the benchmarks.

Do variance reports: The task is to complete reports for the project team on variances of standards and benchmarks as found in inspections and audits. The task uses the data gathered by QC as to method for writing variance reports. Other data would include when they should be completed, why they should be written, and for whom they should be given.

Perform random inspections: It is an independent evaluation or test of part of a project's component by qualified personnel. It is a partial audit. The task includes using QC criteria and doing this task before milestones or critical events.

Identify variances and causes: Anytime this task is performed all related estimates (time, costs, and resources) have to be considered.

Perform audits: It is an independent evaluation or test of some component of the project by qualified personnel. It is more complete than an inspection. An audit is accomplished at a milestone or major event for the listed items.

Identify variances and causes: Anytime this task is performed all related estimates (time, costs, and resources) have to be considered.

Other support groups: Examples of other support groups are Marketing and Human Resources. These groups are only audited as to their performance based on the Scope Plan.

Vendors:

Review RFP responses: The task is to assist in the analysis of any RFP response as to how it reflects the stated requirements and criteria in the RFP.

Analyze performance history: The task is to analyze performance data to ensure that the vendor has demonstrated at the level of work required by the RFP.

Confirm validation process: The task is to verify the vendor's stated validation process from the RFP response.

Confirm testing process: The task is to verify the vendor's stated testing process from the RFP response.

Confirm dependency usage: The task is to validate or test stated dependencies.

Consistency validation: The task is to ensure what is stated in any document is used consistently through the other listed documents. The baseline in all cases is the Scope Plan.

Baseline Plan: This task is to validate or test for any deviations based on criteria from this plan.

Field Introduction: The task is to assist in the process as given in the Trial (Beta) Strategy.

Validate change management process: The task is to validate the change process as to how it is being be managed in accordance with the defined project standards and benchmarks.

Validate update process: The task is to validate the update process as to how it is being be managed in accordance with the defined project standards and benchmarks.

Validate slippage usage: The task is to validate the slippage management process as to it is being managed in accordance with the defined project standards and benchmarks.

Do feedback reports: The task is to feedback report any task listed in this checklist as required by the project team or relevant quality standards.

Assistance resource leveling: The task is to assist in leveling, that is the technique to smooth out peaks and valleys for the use of resources in a Project Schedule.

Analyze logistics criteria: The analysis is to validate that the criteria are being used so the logistics process is getting the correct resource to the correct location at the correct time.

Assist in model development: The task is to use the criteria as established by QC to assist in modeling or simulation. A model is a theoretical environment with as much data as possible to reflect reality adequately for decision making. Simulation is a process to imitate the physical components of the informational system.

Validate and test deliverables: A deliverable is a clearly defined project result, product, or service. It is an outcome. This task is to ensure that all deliverables as defined in the project goals are as promised in the Scope plan. Any deviations are to be reported to the project team.

10RISKF CHECKLIST FOR RISK MANAGEMENT TASKS

First line of defense, basic parameter definition:

1. What are the criteria for a risk?

2. Who defines the risk criteria?

3. When are the risk criteria applied?

4. Where in the project process are risk criteria applied?

5. How are the risk criteria applied?

6. Why has the potential risk happened?

Second line of defense, risk category identification:

1. Customer
2. Delivery
3. Equipment
4. People
5. Physical
6. Scope
7. Technology
8. Vendor

Third level of defense, detailing the process:

1. How does a contingency plan impact risk management?
2. How does cost estimates impact risk management?
3. How will the risk management tasks be funded?
4. What are the direct-cost estimates for risk management?
5. What are the documentation requirements for risk management?
6. What are the essential project tasks for managing risks?
7. What are the resources required for risk management?
8. What are the skills and their levels required for risk management?
9. What are the time estimates for risk management?
10. What are the training requirements for risk management?
11. What procedures, benchmarks, standards, or policies govern risk management?
12. Where in the project budget is risk management allocated?
13. Where in the project process will there be assessments for risks?
14. Where in the project schedule are there appropriate links from the quality control schedule?
15. Who (an individual or a group) is responsible for managing risks?

Fourth line of defense, use of model and simulations:

> Statistical models
> Simulations
> Risk assessments
> Fifth line of defense, performance criteria identification:

1. Acceptable plus or minus measurable variances

2. Assumptions

3. Audit criteria

4. Communications criteria

5. Confidence levels

6. Constraints

7. Criticality criteria

8. Dependency management

9. Distortion possibilities

10. Effectiveness

11. Efficiency

12. Logistics criteria

13. Qualitative impacts

14. Quantitative impacts

10RISKI INSTRUCTIONS FOR A RISK MANAGEMENT TASKS CHECKLIST

These instructions should be done twice. The first time is to define risk management, while the second time is to define opportunity management. This is done by replacing the word "risk" with "opportunity."

First line of defense, basic parameter definition: Use the responses for other checklists and ensure that there is consistency among the responses. The responses to the first fourth questions should be stated in a risk management section of the Scope Plan.

1. What are the criteria for a risk? An example response, a criterion for a risk is in the event that the confidence level for a pessimistic scenario might become greater than 80 per cent.

2. Who defines the risk criteria? An example response, the project team with assistance by members of the IS quality team do the defining.

3. When are the risk criteria applied? An example response, risk criteria are applied by Quality Management Group with consent of the project team.

4. Where in the project process are risk criteria applied? An example response, the location is determined by the negative degree of not meeting standards and benchmarks for "X" number of interrelated tasks or to the critical path.

5. How are the risk criteria applied? An example response, risk criteria are applied as a part of the quality management process.

6. Why has the potential risk happened? The response to question should include what, when, where, and how. It should not include an individual whom.

Second line of defense, risk category identification: When the phrase risk criteria is used, it means a set of criteria. The listed areas must be considered in completing a set of risk criteria. Examples for each are given as a starting point. Each operational area and the critical path must be reviewed for these risk areas.

1. Customer

   - Financial support becomes unavailable
   - Not participating in agreed upon reviews
   - Responses to questions are not timely
   - New interpretations to goals
   - Skill resources availability degrades

2. Delivery

   - Product does not meet functional requirements according to benchmarks, standards or the project goals
   - Product has incompatibility issues
   - Product has interoperability issues
   - Product has portability issues

- Product's capacity exceeds available capacity
- Product's response time is inadequate

3. Equipment
   - Does not meet specifications
   - Limited availability
   - Missed delivery date

4. People
   - Lacking in skills required
   - Not available at time required
   - Not available because of job change

5. Physical
   - Critical computers or hardware failure
   - Data stolen
   - Facility lost through a catastrophe
   - Virus infects some critical data

6. Scope
   - Customer identifies the need for additional effort
   - New requirements are identified during development
   - An operational area introduces a new function that is not been approved by the project team

7. Technology
   - Technical assumptions are not factual
   - Technical constraints cannot be overcome
   - Technology is not understood clearly
   - Technology is too new

8. Vendor
   - Financial failure
   - Not participating in agreed-upon reviews
   - Responses to questions is not timely
   - New interpretations of support and goals
   - Skill resources availability degrades

Third level of defense, detailing the process:

1. How does a contingency plan impact risk management? An example response, the contingency plan should minimize the effects of padding. There should be a determination of the possible amount of padding.

2. How does cost estimates impact risk management? An example response, shoddy cost estimates impact the Project Budget and potential funding requirements. Thus, there need to be a part of any estimate review a consideration of risk impacts.

3. How will the risk management tasks be funded? An example response, risk management tasks will be funded from the contingency fund.

4. What are the direct-cost estimates for risk management? An example response, direct-cost estimates for any full- or part-time employees and the funding are found in the contingency plan.

5. What are the documentation requirements for risk management? An example response, documentation requirements might be either in the form of project or customer documents and the documentation that gives the specifics on the management of an identified potential risk.

6. What are the essential tasks for managing risks? An example response, the essential tasks are defined in accordance with the first and second lines of defense as formulated using the Checklist for Risk Management Tasks.

7. What are the resources required for risk management? An example response, the general resources are all stakeholders, but specific resources are the project manager, the project administrative team, and identified members of the Quality Management function.

8. What are the skills and their levels required for risk management? An example response, originally skills levels are determined by the areas with the highest potentials of risk. Second, skills levels have to be determined when a specific risk is identified and possible solutions have been defined.

9. What are the time estimates for risk management? An example response, the time estimates are blocks of time with funds in the contingency plan and noted as special events in the Project Schedule.

10. What are the training requirements for risk management? An example response, the training requirements are to have a person or persons who can create risk models and simulations, and use risk analysis techniques and tools.

11. What procedures, benchmarks, standards, or policies govern risk management? An example response, a part of the Quality Management process is to collect and use procedures, benchmarks, standards, or policies that govern risk management.

12. Where in the project budget is risk management allocated? An example response, risk management costs are allocated in the budget line for contingency.

13. Where in the project process will there be assessments for risks? An example response, at the completion of any major operational milestones, there should be a review of the status of that milestone's interrelated tasks for potential risks.

14. Where in the project schedule are there appropriate links from the quality management schedule? An example response, the links are determined by the project team and by assistance of the Quality Management function.

15. Who (an individual or a group) is responsible for managing risks? An example response, everyone is responsible for identifying risks, but the project manager is ultimately responsible for managing and solving risks.

Fourth line of defense, use of model and simulations:

Statistical model: This type of model use mathematical distributions to define the performance of an activity or task.

Simulation: It is a process to imitate the physical components of your informational system.

Risk analyses: It is a technique, tool, or method for assessing either quantitatively or qualitatively (or both) the impacts of an identified risk.

Fifth line of defense, performance criteria identification:

1. Acceptable plus or minus measurable variances: It is any deviation from the planned work whether it is costs, time, or resources.

2. Assumption: It is a prediction that something will be true, either an action or an event that ensures project success. A characteristic of a risk is for a positive assumption to fail.

3. Audit criteria: Criteria developed for an independent evaluation or test of the some component of the project by qualified personnel to determine variances.

4. Communications criteria: Criteria used to define the best method for using the communications process for different categories of risks. This means determining the who that gives and receives the information on a potential risk, what data is to be given, when there is to be communication, and how the information is to be given (e-mail or a briefing).

5. Confidence levels: A percentage level for a scenario for a pessimistic, realistic, or optimistic scenario to occur as described should be given.

6. Constraint: It is a parameter, limitation or a boundary for the project plan such as the budget or the schedule. A characteristic of a risk is for a task to go negatively beyond a constraint.

7. Criticality criteria: They are used to determine if a position on the team where the individual in this situation has skills; usually technical that if not available to the project puts the project at risk.

8. Dependency management: This management type is concerned with nonadherence to start-end, start-start, and end-start dependencies and how this may generate risks.

9. Distortion possibilities: It is the misrepresentation of the situation whether it is a fact, experience, or a feeling.

10. Effectiveness: It is the attained measure of quality to complete the activity or event. It is also the skill set required to define goals and to accomplish them.

11. Efficiency: It is the measurement of output based on amount of input. It is also the skill set the can accomplish with a minimum of input to get a maximum of output.

12. Logistics criteria: They are used to define the process of getting the correct resource to the correct location at the correct time.

13. Qualitative impacts: Task performance must be identified as to how well it is being performance. Because a task is supposedly completed does not necessarily mean it was done correctly. This type of failure can generate long-range failures.

14. Quantitative impacts: The amount of resources that went into the completion of a task may be excessive. A determination needs to be done to determine if a potential risk has been generated.

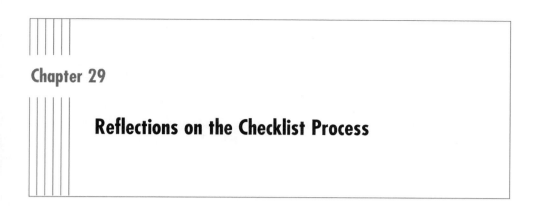

Chapter 29

Reflections on the Checklist Process

This chapter briefly gives reflections that go beyond those given in Section 1A and summarizes the fundamental directions of the section. This chapter is more a jumping off point for further efforts in the realm of the IS project management process. It is a taste of other views of the potential.

In this chapter, you develop knowledge on how to do your reflecting on the IS project management process. You are shown that while you can be lead to the drinking trough, you need to decide how much you are going to drink, if any.

BASIC POINTS FOR USING CHECKLISTS

The basic points in the use of the checklists as found in Chapter 28A and discussed in Section 1A are:

- Garbage in, garbage out is more than a cliché.
- Project managers use the checklists to define tasks based on resource, time, and cost estimates.
- Operational managers use the checklists to define activities.
- The essential test of responses to the checklists is to eliminate or minimize shoddy resource, time, and cost estimates.
- Responses should be consistent and to the level of detail so they are workable.
- The responses to the instructions are based answers to six basic questions: Why? What? Who? When? Where? How?

- All estimates have to be stated in three forms: pessimistic, realistic, and optimistic.
- Padding is a no, no; but contingency is a yes, yes.
- Do not use the words "good" or "bad" for a characteristic of an estimate, but "valid" or "invalid" in accordance with standards and benchmarks.
- The checklists consider all the major parts of the IS infrastructure: hardware, software, network support, interoperability, reliability, scalability, effectiveness, and efficiency.
- The checklists shall be used to write the major management documents of the project: Scope Plan, Activity Plan, Resource Plan, Project Schedule, and Project Budget. Other documents such as the Marketing Plan feed into these management documents.
- Using a simple application for creating forms, you can design and develop many local forms to gather specific data.
- These checklists reflect the types of data required for designing an effective forms management program.
- The instructions reflect the assumptions and constraints for the data to be collected.
- Instructions for forms are nearly forgotten by all groups except the IRS.
- The responses to the checklists for quality management and risk management are primarily summaries of responses to these functions in earlier discussed checklists.
- If the ultimate answer to the project viability questions is no, then any additional effort is ridiculous.
- It takes more time to redo the responses to a checklist a second time than doing it correctly the first time.
- Use the checklists as tools, not as the gospel, since they were developed based on one person's experiences and project management skills.
- The use of the checklists is impacted by the skill set or sets of the user.

SKILL SETS AND THE CHECKLISTS

A skill set here first means the grouping of a set of management skills such as administrating, communicating, organizing, planning, and, writing. Second, the set is labeled in accordance how they used. There are many labels such as:

- Boss
- Dictator
- Facilitator
- Guru
- Indian chief
- Mentor
- Negotiator
- Organizer
- Salesperson

For more details on these labels see Management Skills for IT Professionals (Prentice Hall, 2001).

An argument is made here that a person's basic skill set affects how the checklists will be used. For example, a boss or dictator type will do the "necessary" responses or ignore the checklists and then present the responses as the way the project will be done.

To further this idea the below discussion very briefly looks in more detail at four of the above listed skill sets.

First, the organizer is concerned with the structure of the project as to process, people, time, equipment, and materials. The following are example questions an organizer might ask when using the checklists:

- How does the stated organization found in the responses differ from the actual organization?

- How might the checklists be used to identify organizational forces?
- What are the responses that handle organization interrelationships?
- What kind of organization does quality management?
- What organization does the estimates?
- What type of team organization should exist?
- When does the project team respond to the checklists?
- Where does the customer fit into the checklist process?
- Why does the organization need to consider all the points on each checklist?
- Why does the project need a risk management (place any other name here) group?

Second, the negotiator should use skills that result in "win-win" situations that are critical to achieving project goals. The negotiator views the responses as a contract or a "treaty." Some of the questions a negotiator might ask are:

- How do the responses define the issues?
- How do the responses define all the stakeholders' requirements, needs, or wants?
- How do the responses prepare for further negotiations?
- What are the essential trade-off potentials?
- What are the dynamics of negotiating?
- What is the communications process for negotiating the responses?
- What is the difference between an activity and a task negotiation?
- When do is a pessimistic or optimistic scenario accepted rather than a realistic scenario?
- When is a response to a checklist negotiable?
- Why should a set of responses be negotiated on a given point?

Third, the facilitator is probably a role that you play everyday of the project. To facilitate means to "oil the project's components to achieve effective and efficient results". The facilitator considers how the checklist process can be used to make the project management process easier. Example questions of a facilitator might include:

- How are the checklists to be used to enhance facilitation?
- How do I facilitate conflict resolutions over responses to the checklists?
- How do I handle the push and pull of interrelations that affect responses?
- How do I use facilitators to get valid responses?
- How do the responses create an environment for facilitating?
- How the responses except more than "touching and feeling"?
- What are the potential obstacles to successful facilitation?
- What form of communications has to be done to ensure consistency in the responses?
- What is facilitating used to get desired responses to the checklist?
- When should there be times to facilitate criticisms of the checklist process?

Fourth, the salesperson is a common role that you play during a project but you think to yourself that I am never a salesperson! Incorrect, you must sell your ideas to the team and you must sell the team's ideas to other project stakeholders. A salesperson-type manager might ask the following questions:

- How do I develop a selling strategy directed at the customer on the responses?
- How do I handle resistance to the responses?
- How do I identify the complexity of selling my ideas?
- How do I prepare a sale to upper level management?
- What are the components of a sale on using the checklist process?
- What are there differences between an individual and a group sale on the responses?
- What does it mean to be a salesperson and the project manager?
- What group relationships are important in trying to sell the checklist process?
- When do I use selling to resolution conflicts?
- Why is selling a part of the day-to-day checklist process?

Is there a skill set unique to an IS manager? Of course there is! What drives an IS manager beyond being a masochist? An IS manager uses such words as network, optimization, software, applications, hardware, and so forth. The use of these words implies a certain view of reality. As any other functions in a company, IS has a jargon or do the people in the other functions speak strangely? In comparison to the other skill sets, here are questions an IS manager might ask until shifting into another role:

- How can IS group responses be given priority over other responses?
- How shall technical consultant be used in developing the responses?
- How should the information in the IS databases be used to frame the responses?
- How should the responses be written to ensure the proper use of IS personnel and resources?
- How will non-IS personnel be able to respond properly to the checklists?
- What impact will the responses have on the network's interoperability and scalability?
- What impacts will the project the general IS production flow?
- When should "outsiders" give responses to the checklists?
- Why do there have to be non-technical responses?
- Why should the checklist process be used?

Five positions have been presented. Is any one of them completely correct? No! However, as an IS manager, you must comprehend that this is a critical area of human dynamics if you are to be an effective project manager. No project that impacts the company is purely IS driven.

Glossary

The following terms have been defined as essential or supportive to the project management process and are used to develop forms and their instructions in various contexts in Chapter 1A–10A. The defined term is given in bold type; its number of the chapters in which the term is used, enclosed in parentheses. For example, to acquire a comprehensive coverage of the word "estimate", you would examine how it used in context in Chapters 1A–9A.

Ability is the capacity to achieve or to perform; it is enhanced through training (3A)

Accountability is the act of accepting the responsibility for the results of an act whether it is a success or failure. The usual form is "I accept responsibility for the failure," or "The team accepts responsibility for the success." (9A, 10A)

An **action plan** is the description of what is required to be completed and when it is to be completed. (4A–6A)

An **activity** at the operational level (a task at the tactical level) is the effort required to achieve a measurable result that uses time and resources. (2A, 3A, 7A, 9A)

The **Activity Plan** is a set of definitions. A definition includes the task constraints from the Scope Plan. (3A–6A)

Activity planning is documenting a plan that establishes constraints and assumptions for any action taken during the project process. (3A)

Activity sequencing is the determination of a logical order of activities or tasks that are used in developing a realistic and achievable schedule. (3A, 5A, 6A)

Advising is giving general rather than specific directions, evaluating, giving an option, or instructing. (9A)

An **assumption** is a prediction that something will be true, either an action or an event that ensures project success, such as, "There will be identified potential risks, but somehow they will be overcome." (1A–10A)

An **audit** is a formal study of the project as a whole, or a project's component, as to status (progress and results), costs, and procedures. ((2A, 3A, 9A)

Authority is the investment in managing and controlling a series of tasks such as a project. For example, the critical statement the strategic manager has to make is "The project manager has to authority to make all decisions required to achieve a successful project." (1A, 2A, 8A)

A **baseline plan** is the initial approved point from which any deviations will be determined using standards and benchmarks. (2A, 4A, 6A–9A)

A **benchmark** is specific technical level of excellence. (1A–4A, 7A, 9A)

The **Budget** is a plan where costs are organized into debits and credits (expenses and revenues). It is a formal plan that uses a chart of accounts to give structure to estimates for expenses and revenues. (2A, 7A, 8A)

Budgeting is entering cost estimates into a formal financial structure. (3A, 7A, 8A)

The **Business Affiliate Plan** provides information when the project or a part of the project is to be the responsibility of a third-party developer. (2A)

The **Business Justification** is the general rationale for making the financial investment. (2A, 7A, 8A)

The **Business Justification Update** document ensures that the current view of the implementation of any project goals have performance criteria to meet previous commitments and management expectations. (7A, 8A)

A **checklist** is an organized list, possibly a standard of action that usually has to be followed in sequence to accomplish a specified goal. However, a checklist can be as simple as a set of options for answering the question "Have I considered the following items for this activity or task?" (1A, 2A, 3A)

The **Commercial Specification** is an evolution of the Business Justification. It identifies the market need and gives adequate requirement and limitation data for the design and development group(s). (2A, 7A, 8A)

Communication is oral or written transfer of data or information between individuals. (2A, 3A)

Communications is the process of getting the correct data to the correct person at the correct time in a cost-effective mode. (2A, 3A)

A **confidence level** is the acceptance level of risk usually determined statistically by a percentage of time or cost. (2A, 10A)

A **constraint** is a parameter, limitation, or boundary for the project plan such as the Budget or the Schedule. (1A–3A, 5A, 6A, 9A, 10A)

A **consultant** is a person from outside the normal resource pool with experience on solving a specific project issue. The consultant usually works from a biased position. (1A–4A)

The **Content Agreement** is the written "contract" between the development group and the marketing group as to the content and functions of the project. (2A, 4A)

Contingency is the rational preparation for change. (2A, 4A -6A, 8A, 10A)

A **contingency plan** is the preparation for a pessimistic scenario to become reality. (4A–6A, 8A–10A)

Control is the monitoring of progress and the checking for variances in the plan. (1A, 3A, 9A)

Corporate values are a common set of beliefs held by the corporate stakeholders about their business environment. (2A)

Cost is the amount to be paid or paid for a resource. Lost time does have a cost. (7A)

A **cost-benefit analysis** is the development of a ratio to determine if a project is financially viable. (1A, 2A, 7A, 8A)

Cost estimating is the process of establishing or defining the amount to be budgeted for a task based on constraints and assumptions from the project goals for the duration of the task, the average skills required for completing the task, and the resources required for completing the task. (3A, 7A, 8A)

Creativity is the skill to take apparently unrelated data and to synthesize them into meaningful information. (4A)

A **critical activity** or task if not completed means project failure. (1A–7A, 9A, 10A)

A **critical path** is when there is no available time for the slippage of the activity or task (that is no slack time). (2A, 3A, 5A, 6A)

The **critical path method** (CPM) in its simplest form, is selecting the "must" activities or tasks, and doing them in the shortest possible amount of time, and within the shortest duration. CPM is a network diagramming technique and can be used to estimate the project's earliest completion by establishing the longest series of activities. (2A, 5A, 6A)

Criticality is a position on the team where the individual in this situation has specific skills usually technical, that if not available to the project, puts the project at risk. (4A, 10A)

A **cross-functional team** is the most common type of team for a corporate IS project, and includes many technical and support groups with a multiple set of skills, ideas, goals, attitudes, and so forth. (2A)

The **Customer Documentation Strategy** provides how timely, high-quality project documentation becomes available. There really is a triad in quality: control, documentation, and training. (2A)

A **deliverable** is a clearly defined project result, product, or service. (1A–3A, 5A–7A, 9A)

Dependency means that a task has to be completed before a succeeding task can be completed. For example, coding has to be completed before code testing can be completed. (2A, 4A–7A, 9A, 10A)

The **Design and Development Plan** drives the project Integration Plan that captures all major design and development deliverables and milestones for management tracking and reporting. (2A, 5A–8A)

Distortion is the misrepresentation of the situation whether it is a fact, experience, or feeling. (10A)

Duration is the total involved time of an activity or task, including production-time and wait-time. (3A, 5A–7A)

Effectiveness is the attained measure of quality to complete the activity, task, or event. It is also the skill required to define goals and to accomplish them. (3A, 4A, 10A)

Efficiency is the measurement of output based on amount of input. It is also the skill that can accomplish maximum output with a minimum of input. (3A, 4A, 10A)

The **end-end dependency** means that an activity or a task cannot end until another activity has also ended. (3A)

The **end-start dependency** means that an activity or a task must end before another can start. (3A, 5A, 6A)

An **estimate** is a guess based on opinion, or a forecast based on experience. Cost, time, and resource estimates are the foundations for project planning. (1A–9A)

An **event** is a point in time such as the start or end of an activity or a task. (2A, 3A, 5A, 6A)

Expectation is a stated project goal that can become a perceived undocumented result. (1A–3A, 9A, 10A)

Extrapolation modeling is the theoretical process of extending historical data. (7A, 8A)

Feedback, an activity that should be held on a regular basis, in which the status of the person being evaluated can be clearly stated based on measurable standards or benchmarks. (2A, 3A, 9A)

The **Field Introduction Requirements** document reflects the strategy and detailed plans to verify conformance to specification and functionality as defined in the Project Specification. (2A, 4A, 7A)

A **Gantt chart** is a visual presentation, using a horizontal bar chart that shows activities or tasks against time. It is named after its developer, Henry Laurence Gantt. (3A, 6A)

A **gate** is another term for milestone or a major project event. (2A, 3A, 6A, 8A)

Goal characteristics have to be measurable, specific, and potentially possible. (1A–3A)

A **group** is two or more individuals with corporate identity that is considered an entity. (2A)

Headcount is a factor used by business managers in planning an annual budget but should not be used by project managers. (2A–4A, 7A, 8A)

A **histogram** is the opposite of a Gantt chart because vertical bars are used to represent values. (6A)

Information system project management is a documented parallel process within a set schedule and within a defined budget, with available resources and skills to achieve defined user expectations for a networking environment. The networking environment's primary function is to transmit data among human users. (1A)

The **Initial Budget Estimates** provides a view of the expected development costs, which are usually based on the Preliminary Project Specification. This document is updated in the Project Cost Update. (2A, 3A, 7A, 8A)

The **Initial Funding Requirements** document is for monitoring and reporting project costs at each major phase of implementation. It should include comparisons to the original funding document used to establish financial targets and expected milestones and deliverables. This document can also be included in the Project Cost Update. (2A, 3A, 7A, 8A)

Innovation is a significant change or breakthrough. (1A)

The **International Organization for Standardization** (ISO) is a consortium that sets standards in a variety of areas. (2A, 4A, 9A)

Interoperability is the degree to which the various network components work with each other successfully. (1A–3A)

ISO 9000 is a quality system standard for any product, service, or process. (2A, 9A)

ISO 9001 is a quality system standard for design, production, and installation of a product or service. (2A, 9A)

ISO 9002 is a quality system model for quality assurance in production and installation. (2A, 9A)

ISO 9003 is a quality system model for quality assurance in final inspection and testing. (2A, 9A)

ISO 9004 is a set of quality management guidelines for any organization to use to develop and implement a quality system. (2A, 9A)

Lag-time is the time between two activities or tasks because of their natures. (3A, 5A, 6A)

Lead-time is the overlapping time of two activities or task. (3A, 5A, 6A)

A **learning curve** is a graphical representation of repetitive tasks that, when done on a continuous basis, lead to a reduction in activity duration, resources, and costs. (2A–7A)

Leveling is the technique used to smooth out peaks and valleys in the use of resources. (3A, 4A, 6A, 7A, 9A)

Line-staff conflicts are differences of opinion and ideas between horizontal management levels. (9A, 10A)

Logistics is the process of getting the correct resource to the correct location at the correct time. (1A–10A)

Management is the process of working with people, resources, equipment, and materials to achieve organizational goals. (1A)

A **management review** is a regularly scheduled performance review. (2A, 4A–7A, 9A, 10A)

Management team is a supervisory team that coordinates broad issues that affect the corporation. (1A)

The **Market Analysis Report** documents and verifies market opportunities and justifies the features, services, and applications for the project goals. (1A–3A, 7A)

A **milestone** is a clearly defined date of start or date of 100% completion. (2A, 3A, 5A, 6A, 9A)

A **model** is a theoretical environment with as much data as possible to reflect reality adequately for decision-making. (1A–3A, 9A)

A **node** is a network event that is achieved or is not achieved. A milestone is a node type. (2A, 3A)

An **objective** is a set of measurable goals to achieve a defined target, if not achieved, has critical results. (1A–6A)

An **operational manager** is the person that handles the day-to-day operations or activities for a specific functional group or area that has been defined in the project plan. (2A, 3A)

An **opportunity** is a situation that will positively affect the project in time, money, resources, or all three in a significant manner. (1A–3A, 9A, 10A)

An **optimistic estimate** is an assumption that holds that everything will go as planned. (3A–9A)

An **organization** is an entity created to achieve what the separate individuals could not accomplish. (1A)

An **organization chart** is normally a visual representation of who reports to whom. It shows the hierarchical and perhaps functional relationships among organizational groups. The project organization chart must include the core project responsibilities of each team member. (2A, 3A, 8A)

Organizational culture is a common set of assumptions, principles, processes, and structures held or used by members of a corporation, company, or even a project team. (2A)

Padding is an informal action, such as adding time or cost to an estimate, that should not take place. Any such estimates should be formalized in a contingency plan. (2A–4A, 6A–9A)

A **path** is a sequence of lines within a network diagram with the most important is labeled critical. The critical path is the timeline of the necessary work to be completed in the minimum amount of time. (3A)

Performance is the measurable level of action to achieve a measurable project goal. It is the act or level of work demonstrated and judged based on identified skill level. (2A–4A, 7A, 9A, 10A

A **pessimistic estimate** is an assumption that if something can go wrong, it will. (3A–9A)

A **phase** is a project segment such as planning, designing, and developing. (2A, 3A)

PMI stands for the Project Management Institute, a professional organization that studies and promotes project management. (2A, 9A)

Portability is a characteristic of software. It is the degree to which the software can be transferred from one environment to another. (1A–3A)

Process is a systematic and sequential set of activities (tasks) to achieve a set of measurable goals. (1A–3A, 6A, 9A)

A **program** is a type of recurring project, such as the annual budget, not to be confused with a set of programming code. (1A, 2A)

Program Evaluation and Review Technique (PERT) was developed for the United States Department of Defense in the late 1950s. Specifically it was developed by the consulting firm of Booz, Allen, and Hamilton for the U.S. Navy's Polaris submarine project (Polaris Weapon System). It combines statistics and network diagrams. (2A, 9A)

A **project** is an organized set of tasks to reach a measurable outcome within a specified duration. (1A–3A)

A **project budget** is the duration (work-time plus the wait-time) of the project cycle. (2A)

The **Project Cost Updates** document updates the initial project cost estimates at each major phase of implementation with comparison to the Initial Budget Estimate. (2A, 7A, 8A)

A **project's duration** is the total number of calendar days involved from start to end, including the project manager's activities in closing the project. (2A, 3A, 5A, 6A)

Project management has many aliases including program management, product management, and construction management. In all cases, it is the managing, controlling, and integrating of tasks, resources, time, and costs to achieve a defined measurable outcome within a specified duration. (1A)

The **project manager** is the person with overall responsibility for managing and controlling the project tasks (defined and undefined) to achieve a measurable outcome within a specified schedule and budget. (1A, 2A)

The **Project Proposal** is a formal response to the Commercial Specification that describes the requirements for a project. (2A)

The **Project Specification** is a formal response to the Commercial Specification that specifies the requirements for a project. (2A)

The **Project Support Plan** ensures that the project is supportable in a market environment. This plan should include a process for customer support. (2A, 4A, 7A)

A **project team** is an organization that is put together to achieve a specific set of measurable goals within a specific time and with limited resources, equipment, and materials. (1A, 2A)

Quality assurance is based on performance. It is the establishing of performance standards, then measuring and evaluating project performance against these standards. This component of quality management considers measurable deviations in performance during a project. (1A, 2A, 9A)

A **quality audit** is an independent evaluation or test of some component of the project by qualified personnel. (2A–7A, 9A, 10A)

Quality control is the component of quality management that considers the system or development processes of a project. It is the tasks used to meet standards through the gathering of performance information, inspecting, monitoring, and testing. (1A, 2A, 9A)

Quality management uses control and assurance to prevent risks and if a risk occurs to minimize it. (2A, 9A)

The **Quality Plan** defines the roles of quality control and assurance in all phases of the project process. (2A, 3A, 9A)

A **realistic estimate** is an assumption that there will probably be a few difficulties, but with compromise, the difficulties will be overcome. (1A, 3A–9A)

A **resource** is anything that supports the project. This includes, in general terms, money, skills, materials, time, facilities, and equipment. (1A–4A, 7A)

Resource planning is establishing support requirements for a project as to costs, availability, start-date and end-date (length of time for use plus duration), and technical specifications. (1A, 3A–6A)

Responsibility is the obligation or accountability given through assignment to complete a specific activity or task. (2A)

A **risk** is a performance error that can have a significant or disastrous impact on the success of a project or major task. It is more than a problem; its effect can have an adverse or disastrous consequence on the project's outcome. (1A–3A, 9A, 10A)

Risk analysis is a technique, tool, or method for assessing either quantitatively or qualitatively (or both) the impacts of an identified risk or a potential risk identified through a scenario. (4A–6A, 10A)

Risk management is the task where you identify a risk, assess a risk, and allocate resources to resolve the risk. (10A)

Role is a skill set with a label that perhaps explains the reasons for the actions and behavior of the actor. (2A)

Scalability is to what degree a network can be enhanced without a major change in design. (1A–3A)

A **scenario** is a set of possibilities that could happen to cause a risk. (9A, 10A)

The **Schedule** is the duration of the project, including production-time and wait-time. It is also a production plan for the allocation of tasks with deadlines. (1A, 2A, 5A, 6A, 8A)

Scheduling is the task that formalizes the time estimates within a calendar structure. It is an integration of sequencing tasks, resource planning, cost estimating, and time estimating. (3A, 5A–7A)

Scope is the amount of work and resources (skills, materials, and equipment) required for project completion. (1A, 2A)

Scope defining is extending the measurable goals to become general procedures with measurable constraints and viable assumptions. (2A)

The **Scope Plan** is the strategic view of the constraints and assumptions of the project as developed by the project team. (2A, 5A, 6A)

Scope planning is defining the project goals and the performance expectations of the goals in measurable terms, and getting agreement on them. (2A)

Simulation is a process to imitate the physical components of your informational system. Simulation has a counterpart–emulation. (9A)

Skill level is a factor used by a project manager in planning the project's Budget rather than using headcount. (1A–4A, 7A 8A)

Slack time is the difference between earliest and latest (start or finish) times for an activity, a task, or an event. (3A, 5A, 6A)

Slippage (budget) is when a budget item is overspent. (3A, 8A)

Slippage (time) is expected when you know about it before the due date; it is unexpected when you learn about it after-the-fact such as after the due date. (3A, 5A, 6A, 8A)

Specific goals are project goals that are measurable, unambiguous, and match exactly the customer's stated expectations. (1A–3A)

The **sponsor** is the one who provides the resources and the working environment to make possible the achievement of project goals. (1A, 2A)

A **stakeholder** is any person or organization interested in the project. This includes the customer, your boss, you, the team, and interested government regulators. (1A, 2A)

A **standard** is usually an external, industry-accepted document for achieving quality for one or more of the project-defined expected goals. (1A–6A, 9A)

The **start-end dependency** means that an activity or task must begin before another one can end. (3A, 5A, 6A)

The **start-start dependency** means that one activity or a task must start before another. (3A, 5A, 6A)

The **state-change model** is concerned with conditions and events that can change the state of your enterprise network. (3A)

A **Statement of Work** (SOW) is an integrated set of descriptions as to project tasks, goals, risks, and resources to complete a measurable outcome. (1A–3A)

A **strategic manager** heads an area of a corporation that includes the IS project as a part of that person's performance goals. (1A, 2A)

A **system** is an interactive set of activities or groups that form a whole with dynamics that impact all the components. (1A)

The **tactical manager** is the one responsible for the overall flow of the project process so that the strategic goals are met. (1A, 2A)

A **task** is a cohesive work unit that is meaningful for tracking that is a set of activities. Writing a line of code is not a task, but writing a module that handles a specific function is a task. (2A, 3A)

A **team** is a group with a common purpose and with skills that compliment each other. (2A)

The **Third-Party Market Agreement** provides the plans whereby the entire project or a part of the project is to be the responsibility of a third-party developer. (1A, 2A)

The **Third-Party Service Plan** defines how the project is to be serviced by a third-party developer. (2A)

Time estimating is concerned with the duration of an individual activity or groups of related activities (tasks). (3A, 5A, 6A, 7A)

A **trade-off** is an act of balancing project constraints. (2A, 3A, 5A–7A)

The **Training Strategy** shows how training is to be designed, developed, implemented, and verified. (2A)

The **Trial (Beta) Strategy** identifies the software and hardware elements in the project that are a part of any trial. Also the "where," the "when," and the "whom" should be included in the strategy. This provides a clear identification of the testing requirements plus the extent of the resources and capabilities necessary to trial. (2A, 4A, 7A, 9A)

Variance is any deviation from the planned work whether it is cost, time, or resources. (2A, 4A–7A, 9A, 10A)

Index